THOMAS COOK
Travellers

PARIS

D1343207

AA

Produced by AA Publishing

Written by Elisabeth Morris

Series adviser: Melissa Shales

Editor: Helen Douglas-Cooper

The Automobile Association would like to thank Emmanuelle Maudit, Thomas Cook Bankers France.

Edited, designed and produced by AA Publishing.
Maps © The Automobile Association 1993

Distributed in the United Kingdom by AA Publishing, Fanum House, Basingstoke, Hampshire, RG21 2EA.

The contents of this publication are believed correct at the time of printing. Nevertheless, the publishers cannot accept responsibility for errors or omissions, or for changes in details given. Assessments of attractions, hotels, restaurants and so forth are based upon the author's own experience and, therefore, descriptions given in this guide necessarily contain an element of subjective opinion which may not reflect the publishers' opinion or dictate a reader's own experiences on another occasion.

We have tried to ensure accuracy in this guide, but things do change and we would be grateful if readers would advise us of any inaccuracies they may encounter.

A CIP catalogue record for this book is available from the British Library.

ISBN 0 7495 0628 8

Published by The Automobile Association and the Thomas Cook Group Ltd.

This book was produced using QuarkXPress™, Aldus Freehand™ and Microsoft Word™ on Apple Macintosh™ computers.

Colour separation: BPCC Reprographics Ltd, Dunstable

Printed by Edicoes ASA, Oporto, Portugal

Cover picture: *The Tour Eiffel*
Title page: *Typical boulangerie, Montmartre*
Above: *Street artist, place des Vosges*

Contents

Introduction

*F*luctuat nec mergitur, 'she is buffeted by the waves but she does not sink', has been the city's proud motto for over four centuries... and still holds true today.

Through revolutions, wars, foreign occupation and, above all, re-development, Paris has remained true to her image for generation after generation of enthusiastic admirers.

The sheer beauty of the capital conquers first-time visitors. A harmonious ensemble of splendid monuments and elegant domestic architecture provides a unique impression of unity; moreover, everything seems to be in its rightful place from the Madeleine matching the National Assembly across the place de la Concorde to the unobtrusive place Dauphine at the tip of the Ile-de-la-Cité. Yet subtle planning and inspired improvisation are constantly remodelling the seemingly perfect image of Paris and, while pessimists predict that 'it will never be the same again', innovations are enthusiastically accepted by Parisians and outsiders alike. To give but three examples: the Eiffel Tower, which raised such an outcry when it was built a hundred years ago, has become the most familiar landmark of the city; the controversial Centre Pompidou is now the most visited monument; and the Louvre would already seem incomplete without its pyramid.

Spectacular view from the Eiffel Tower

Paris' charm

However, beauty alone does not explain the attraction of Paris for so many. One could argue its vast cultural wealth, the prestige of its *haute couture,* the infinite variety of its cuisine or its long-standing reputation in the field of entertainment. However, its magical appeal is due mainly to an undefinable charm that seems to spring quite unexpectedly from the many facets of everyday life. Ordinary details, no matter how trivial, suddenly seem to acquire a new dimension: it could be a quaint-looking kiosk on a street corner, a white-globed street lamp in the middle of a tiny square, an old-fashioned shop front, the *bouquinistes* (second-hand bookstalls) in the morning mist or just an evocative street name like the rue du Chat-qui-

Pêche (fishing cat street).

Full of contradictions, Paris never ceases to surprise: at once compact and spacious, it can be in turn pompous and modest, quiet and exuberant, cheap and outrageously expensive, enthralling and infuriating depending on the place and the time of day.

The Conciergerie, massive yet graceful

PARIS QUOTES

'Nothing can be compared to Paris.'
From a popular 14th century ballad by Eustache Descamps

'This city without an equal, this summary of France.'
Jean Bertaut (16th century)

'Paris is well worth a Mass!'
Henri IV, when he converted to Catholicism to become King of France

'Whoever looks into the depths of Paris gets dizzy. Nothing so fantastic, nothing so tragic, nothing so superb.'
Victor Hugo

'Paris is like an ocean; you can try to fathom it but you will never know its real depth.'
Honoré de Balzac

'As an artist, a man has no home save in Paris.'
Friedrich Nietzsche

'The last time I saw Paris, her heart was warm and gay,
I heard the laughter of her heart in every street café.'
Oscar Hammerstein

FAMOUS PARISIANS
Fifteen hundred plaques on buildings throughout the city commemorate famous Parisians.

Parisians by birth

Molière, the celebrated playwright at the court of Louis XIV.
George Sand, the romantic novelist, who had a notorious love affair with another Parisian (by adoption), Chopin.
The sculptor, Auguste Rodin, whose house is now a museum.
The Montmartre painter, Maurice Utrillo.
The philosopher Jean-Paul Sartre, an exponent of Existentialism.
The cabaret singer Maurice Chevalier.

Parisians by adoption

The painter Eugène Delacroix, a friend of Sand and Chopin.
Vincent van Gogh, who lived in Montmartre with his brother Theo.
Oscar Wilde, who ended his unhappy life in St-Germain-des-Prés.
Ernest Hemingway, who lived in Paris with fellow Americans during the 1920s and 30s.
Pablo Picasso, one of the founders of cubism.
The Duke and Duchess of Windsor, who lived in the exclusive avenue Foch.

History

52BC
Roman legions conquer the island; the settlement, called Lutetia, prospers through extensive river trading and spreads to the left bank.

cAD250
The martyrdom of the first bishop of the city, Saint-Denis, on Montmartre.

c280
The city is raided by barbarians and the *Parisii* take refuge on the island.

c360
Lutetia is renamed Paris.

451
As the population prepares to flee before the hordes of Attila's Huns, a young girl, called Genevieve, predicts that the town will be spared; she later becomes the patron saint of the city.

508
The first Christian king of the Franks, Clovis, makes Paris his capital.

7th C
King Dagobert is buried in the Basilica of Saint-Denis, a tradition observed by the kings of France for more than eight centuries.

800
Charlemagne is crowned Emperor and chooses Aachen for his capital; Paris slowly declines.

9th C
Repeated Norman raids terrify the population.

1163
The bishop of Paris, Maurice de Sully, decides to build Notre-Dame Cathedral.

1180
King Philippe-Auguste orders a new city wall to be built and commissions the Louvre fortress.

1215
The university of Paris, the first in France, is founded.

1253
Foundation of the Sorbonne.

1364
Charles V builds a new wall round Paris and lays the foundation stone of the Bastille.

1420
At the height of the Hundred Years' War, Paris is occupied by English forces led by Henry V.

1429
Joan of Arc besieges Paris but fails to dislodge the English.

1430
Henry VI of England is crowned king of France.

1436
Charles VII recaptures the city.

1546
Work starts on a new Renaissance palace at the Louvre.

1572
The massacre of Saint-Bartholomew's Day accounts for the death of several thousand Huguenots.

1578-1604
The Pont-Neuf, the oldest extant bridge in Paris, is built.

1594-1610
Work continues on the Louvre and the Tuileries; the first square in Paris (the place des Vosges) is commissioned.

1635
Richelieu founds the French Academy

Late 17th C
Versailles becomes Louis XIV's residence. The king founds Les Invalides.

Early 18th C
The aristocracy moves to the Faubourg St-Germain.

c1760
Louis XV commissions the building of the Ecole Militaire, the Panthéon and the place de la Concorde.

1789
The fall of the Bastille on 14 July marks the beginning of the French Revolution.

1792
The monarchy falls and the First Republic is proclaimed.

1793
Louis XVI goes to the guillotine. The Louvre Museum opens.

1804
Napoleon is crowned Emperor in Notre-Dame.

Early 19th C
The Arc de Triomphe is built, together with several theatres and shopping arcades.

1837
Opening of the first French railway line between Paris and St-Germain-en-Laye.

1841-1845
The 'Thiers' fortifications are built.

1852-1870
Baron Haussmann remodels Paris.

The Eiffel Tower as it appeared in 1889

1870-1871
As a result of the Franco-Prussian war, the Third Republic is proclaimed and the Paris Commune is crushed at the expense of some of the town's finest monuments.

1889
The Eiffel Tower is built for the Exposition Universelle.

1900
The first métro line is opened. Paris becomes an international centre of fashion and entertainment. Montmartre witnesses the birth of modern art.

1914
Paris is saved from German invasion by the Battle of the Marne.

1937
The Palais de Chaillot and Tokyo are built for the Exposition Universelle.

1940
Paris is bombed, then occupied by German troops.

1944
Paris is liberated.

1958
Work starts on La Défense.

1968
During the 'May Events', barricades are put up in the streets.

1969
The Halles central food market is moved to Rungis, outside Paris.

1973
The boulevard périphérique (ring-road) is completed.

1977
The first mayor of Paris since 1871 is elected and the Centre Pompidou is opened.

1986
The Orsay Museum and the Cité des Sciences at La Villette are inaugurated.

1989
A series of impressive celebrations commemorate the bicentenary of the fall of the Bastille, including the inauguration of the Bastille Opera and of the Grande Arche at La Défense.

Geography

*P*aris is situated in northern France, at the centre of a vast natural chalk basin drained by the River Seine and its numerous tributaries, including the Marne and the Oise.

THE ILE-DE-FRANCE

The area surrounding Paris is, as its name suggests, the very 'heart' of France. This privilege goes back to the 6th century, when the region already formed the core of the kingdom of the Franks. Rich agricultural land, green valleys, beautiful forests, a temperate climate, easy communications and the presence of the capital in its centre secured its supremacy over the rest of the country. However, the division of the whole French territory into some 90 *départements* at the end of the 18th century made the region's limits rather difficult to define. It was, for a long time, vaguely referred to as the 'Paris Region' and the name Ile-de-France seemed to

be relegated to history books. However, since 1976, France has been divided into 22 regions, each including several *départements* and the Paris Region has officially been given back its original name Ile-de-France.

An economy in full expansion

The Ile-de-France is an area of great economic wealth, modelled by its illustrious past but definitely looking to the future. It covers only 2.2 per cent of France, but as it accommodates a fifth of the population and has no fewer than five 'new towns', it is by far the most densely populated of all the regions and

The Périphérique defines the city limits

produces over a quarter of the gross national product.

Commerce, transport and service industries are the most developed economic activities and account for nearly three quarters of the jobs. The industrial sector is almost equally strong and produces a quarter of the total industrial wealth of the country. Power generation, electronics, publishing and printing, pharmaceutical products, car and ship-building, as well as food, are the main industries.

Agriculture, on the other hand, although far from negligible and highly efficient, is very much in the background economically speaking, and tends to specialise more and more in the intensive production of cereals, flowers and ornamental plants.

Paris from the Tour Montparnasse

Welcome independence

The Ile-de-France comprises Paris and seven other *départements* clustering round the capital. Since the introduction of gradual decentralisation over the past 20 years, the region has been governed by a *Conseil Régional* consisting of 197 councillors elected for a period of six years, assisted by a *Comité économique et social*, which advises on specific projects.

THE TRUE PARISIAN

The population of Paris has, like that of many large towns, become so cosmopolitan that the notion of 'true Parisian' may seem like a myth! But visitors need have no fear...the true Parisian is still very real.

He or she may originally have come from a different part of France or even from abroad, but once adopted by Paris, becomes a true Parisian: hurrying along the pavements and the métro corridors, hurrying to work and hurrying back home again in the evening, hurrying through life in fact...not particularly amiable, especially if at the wheel of a car, but quick-witted and able to enjoy life intensely for a fleeting moment.

Nothing shocks or even surprises and that would make him or her very tolerant...if there was time!

PARIS

Neatly enclosed within a mostly efficient ringroad, which can be highly frustrating during the rush hour, Paris, dominated by the Seine, covers an area of a mere 105sq km. The population of the capital has now stabilised at just over 2 million inhabitants, which makes it one of the most densely populated cities in the world. During the past 15 years, the tendency has been for people to move out of Paris and settle in other *départements* of the region, which Parisians call *la banlieue* (suburbs). The areas surrounding the capital are officially referred to as *la petite couronne* (the close suburbs) and *la grande couronne* (the outskirts).

Politics

*P*aris owes its unique economic and cultural drive to its long-standing role as capital of France. It took an active part in all the major events of French history, suffering greatly during the more sombre periods of revolution and war, but always recovering and regaining its vitality, wit and artistic taste.

The classically styled Assemblée nationalle, where the lawmaking body of the French parliament sits

The corridors of power

Today there are in France three distinct components of government: the President, the Government and Parliament.

Parliament consists of two houses: the *Assemblée nationale,* elected for five years, sits in the Palais Bourbon facing the place de la Concorde; it discusses and votes on the laws, while the *Sénat,* elected for nine years and housed in the Palais du Luxembourg, has a purely advisory role.

The Government is made up of the Prime Minister, chosen by the President, and a variable number of ministers. Together they are answerable to the *Assemblée nationale* for their policies.

The Prime Minister resides in the Hôtel Matignon, in the Faubourg St-Germain.

The Président de la République, is elected for seven years; he chooses the Prime Minister and presides over cabinet meetings. He is head of the armed forces, has considerable powers in foreign affairs, ensures the independence of the judiciary and may be granted special powers in exceptional circumstances. The Elysée Palace is the President's official residence.

Helping to turn the wheels of power, the political parties and the trade unions are all based in the capital, as are the national newspapers.

Finally, one must not forget the people of Paris who have always shown great interest in the running of national affairs and take an active part in decision-making through frequent street demonstrations and gatherings in public squares.

Embassies from countries all over the world have long been established in the capital, which is also the seat of major international organisations such as UNESCO (United Nations Educational, Scientific and Cultural Organisation) or OECD (Organisation for Economic Co-operation and Development). Paris has lately become the most sought after centre of international congresses in the world, overtaking London and Brussels.

Town and département

At local government level, Paris has, since 1977, enjoyed the unique privilege of being at once a *commune* and a *département*. As a *commune* or municipality, it has an elected mayor chosen by the municipal council; elections are held every six years. The *commune* of Paris is divided into 20 *arrondissements*, each having its own

mayor and working closely with the central municipal authority, which meets at the Hôtel de Ville.

When the Ile-de-France region came into being, the Seine *département,* of which Paris was the main town, and several *départements* surrounding the capital were remodelled and new ones created: with a fifth of the region's total population, Paris became a *département* in its own right, administered by the *Conseil de Paris.* The postal code, specific to addresses within the capital, reflects this duality: it consists of five digits starting with 75 for the *département,* followed by 001 to 020 depending on the *arrondissement.*

Decentralisation

The endowment on the local authority of real powers proved beneficial to the town as it enabled the municipality and the state to share the responsibility of the capital's great architectural heritage and to initiate daring futuristic projects aimed at maintaining Paris' position as one of the major European cities of the 20th century. Even if everything has not always gone smoothly, the results so far are stunning: whole districts, which had become derelict, have been restored (like the Marais) or completely rebuilt (like the Halles) but their traditions have been preserved. At the same time, the renovation of eastern districts, neglected for far too long, was inspired by bold town planning principles with astonishing results: thus La Villette is fast becoming a major cultural attraction.

Excitement over the changing face of Paris is not about to abate, especially since communications and the environment have become very controversial issues in local politics.

Culture

*F*oreigners usually expect to discover in Paris the very essence of French culture and they are right to a certain extent, although provincial French people would not agree, however proud they may be of their capital. Wit, elegance and energy are all to be found in Paris. Parisians are aware that the rest of France is watching them and have always considered this a worthwhile challenge. As a result, they have developed a strong need to innovate as well as a tremendous drive to achieve their goals. This is nowhere more apparent than in the way the city is being gradually steered into the 21st century.

Big sign for a big show in Montparnasse

The changing face of Paris

Systematic restoration work has recently been undertaken, and some buildings have acquired a renewed and original usefulness. The magnificent but obsolete Gare d'Orsay has been renovated in an imaginative way and turned into an art museum, while a glass pyramid lets daylight into the new underground entrance hall of the Louvre Museum. Moreover, for the first time, whole districts have been saved from dereliction with the help of modern techniques; thus the splendour of the past has come to life again in the Marais. At the same time, vast architectural projects have, in the last 20 years, ensured cultural continuity; some of them, such as the Forum des Halles, La Villette and La Défense, are particularly striking. The simplicity of their outlines is enhanced by the quality and beauty of the building materials used.

A certain way of life

Parisians may be fond of new ideas, but they are also conservative and their lifestyle reflects this constant conflict between innovation and tradition. Paris has always been a compact city and Parisians have become used to living in cramped conditions, in blocks of flats that traditionally have six storeys and a *concierge* (caretaker) on the ground floor. Therefore, street life is important to them: local bistros, brasseries and cafés are a favourite meeting-place throughout the day. Open-air markets, where people from different generations and social backgrounds mingle in a colourful display of exuberance, have remained the focal point of many districts.

Furthermore, Parisians have a reputation for trend-setting: a district suddenly becomes fashionable and everyone wants to live in it. This phenomenon is also apparent in two other important aspects of the Parisian life, clothing and food, where there is a definite cosmopolitan influence.

Subtle changes

The traditional way of life is gradually changing as the fabric of the population itself alters: the number of workers in high-tech industries, members of the professional classes and artists is increasing rapidly, while the contrast between wealthy western districts and poorer eastern areas is disappearing. At the same time, the pace of living has considerably quickened, inevitably damaging personal contacts. On the other hand, Paris is becoming truly cosmopolitan, which has brought greater cultural variety to the Parisian scene.

Culture for everyone

Paris is as much as ever a melting-pot of artistic creation and a place where one can never tire of being a spectator, such is the wealth of cultural activities. Music, drama and the visual arts are taught at various levels, from the municipal schools to the national *conservatoires*.

Paris is also the place to visit for those who do not take an active part in culture but thrive on it: there are, of course, prestigious opera houses, concert halls and theatres, but there are also free concerts in many churches all over town and *avant-garde* plays in tiny obscure theatres.

In addition to their permanent collections, museums and art galleries organise temporary exhibitions. The number of libraries is increasing rapidly and there are still a record number of cinemas in spite of fierce competition from television. This brief review of the cultural scene would be incomplete without a special mention of two great multi-purpose cultural centres: the Pompidou Centre and the music and science complex at La Villette.

The stately 16th-century Louvre, now served by its glass-pyramid information centre

Finding your feet

Where next? Here are some pointers

When to go

In summer Paris belongs to the tourists. If you are looking for authenticity, August is the worst month as the city is deserted by Parisians, cultural activities are at a low ebb, quite a few restaurants and shops are closed and, on top of it all, the weather can be uncomfortably close.

Winter has a certain charm with statues and monuments looking stark through the leafless trees, but night falls very quickly. Crowds in the streets reach their peak at Christmas time, which is a particularly lively period. January, with its traditional sales, is a good time for shopping.

However, late spring and early autumn are, on the whole, the most exciting seasons in which to visit Paris: in springtime, parks and gardens are a haven of freshness while the long warm evenings invite you to stroll along the

Seine or watch the sun set the Arc de Triomphe ablaze. There is a holiday spirit in the air which brings smiles and humour into everyday conversation. On the other hand, autumn marks the start of the season, *la rentrée* as the French call it: theatres and opera houses reopen, major exhibitions are announced, new trends in fashion are set and children go back to school; moreover, Parisians are at their friendliest after their holidays spent away from the capital.

First impressions

On arrival, you might take a taxi and be whirled round the place Charles de Gaulle, which continues to be referred to as l'Etoile. This can be a hair-raising experience, but you will quickly come to terms with it when you realise that the *priorité à droite* (priority to vehicles

The Champs Elysées, leading to the Tuileries

Lost? Find help at handy roadside maps

the volume of traffic and the time restrictions on parking.

Therefore, your best course of action is to leave your car in a long-term car park (ask your hotel for information on the nearest one) and take to the streets.

Walking
This is by far the best way to visit the centre as distances are manageable and there are no hills. However, sooner or later, you will need to use some form of public transport.

coming from the right) really works – most of the time, anyway! From then on the pace is set, and you begin to get the feel of the place: Paris is a densely populated, relatively compact city, but careful planning has provided it with wide avenues and two main thoroughfares along the Seine.

Finding your bearings
This is a fairly easy task from almost anywhere, since central Paris is relatively small and some of the familiar landmarks act as beacons: the Sacré Coeur Basilica on top of Montmartre is due north, the Eiffel Tower is to the west and the Montparnasse Tower dominates the southern part of town. Getting hold of a detailed map should be your first move. All street signs show which *arrondissement* you are in and if you look these up in the index of your Paris street plan, it will even give you the nearest métro.

GETTING AROUND
Driving
If you are driving to Paris, you will soon discover that a car is not the best means to explore the French capital because of

THOMAS COOK'S PARIS
Thomas Cook undertook his first-ever trip abroad to the Paris Exhibition in 1855. Because he couldn't get a concession on the short channel crossing he went from Harwich to Brussels, down the Rhine to Strasbourg and then overland to Paris.

The party included four unaccompanied sisters, who later recorded that although criticised for their daring, they felt they could venture anywhere escorted by Mr Cook. This set the pattern for Cook's subsequent tours, which were heavily patronised by unaccompanied women, whose travel horizons would otherwise have been severely limited by Victorian ideas of propriety.

The total cost of the first trip, including expenses, was estimated by one of the sisters as £10 0s 0d.

Paris became a favourite destination for Cook's parties, and remains a major destination today. From late Victorian times Thomas Cook published a guidebook to Paris which became a standard guide until the outbreak of World War II.

Public Transport

The métro, the RER and the buses are part of a very efficient system. The *métro,* short for *métropolitan,* is an underground network of 15 lines covering the whole of the city within the périphérique; trains are frequent, stations are close to one another and there is one flat fare throughout. You can either buy tickets

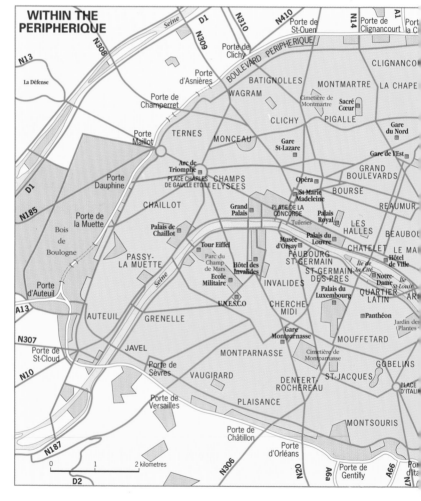

WITHIN THE PERIPHERIQUE

in lots of 10 (a *carnet*) or get a *Paris-Visite* pass for unlimited travel anywhere for a specified number of days; you can combine it with a *Carte Musée-Monuments* (museum pass). Maps of the whole network are posted outside stations and on platforms. You can change from one line to another at intersection points by following the sign *correspondance*. The métro runs daily from 5.30am to 1.15am; buses from 6.30am to either 9pm or 1am (for more information on transport, see the Practical Guide).

Travelling on the métro can be hectic, especially during the rush hour. A journey by bus, on the other hand, is usually an enjoyable experience but don't forget to allow extra time and to ring the bell when you want to get off. The same tickets are used on buses and on the métro, but you may need two on the bus depending on the length of your journey.

The latest arrivals on the Paris street scene are route finders, which look like cash dispensers and are called SITU. They are programmed to work out the quickest way to any destination by one or several means of transport, including walking.

The RER (Réseau Express Régional) is a suburban network of fast trains linked to the métro. The flat-fare system applies only within the city boundaries. The RER has reduced the travelling time between the international airports of Orly and the centre of Paris to about half an hour.

Batobus

This 'riverbus' operates from April to September between the Eiffel Tower and the Hôtel de Ville, stopping at the Musée d'Orsay, the Louvre and Notre-Dame.

Taxis

The best place to get one is from a taxi-rank, headed by the sign *Tête de station*. Drivers accept a maximum of three or four passengers and expect a tip of at least 10 per cent.

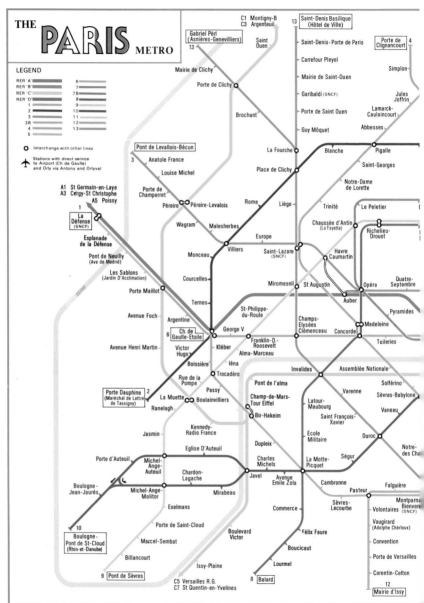

THE PARIS METRO

LEGEND

RER 'A'   6
RER 'B'   7
RER 'C'   7B
RER 'D'   8
1   9
2   10
3   11
3B   12
4   13
5

○ Interchange with other lines

Stations with direct service to Airport (Ch de Gaulle) and Orly via Antony and Orlyval

A1 St Germain-en-Laye
A3 Cergy-St Christophe
A5 Poissy

© TCS

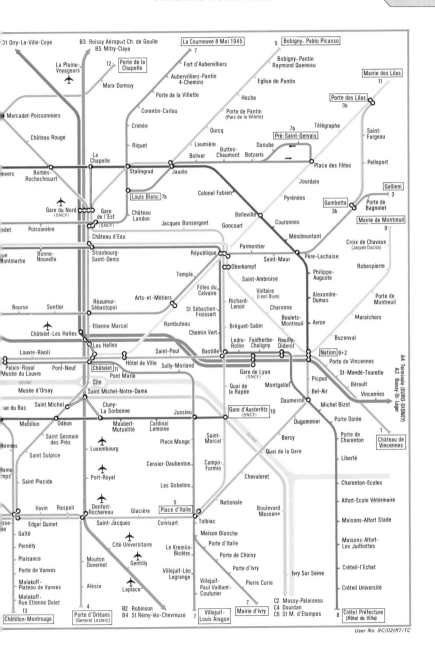

Areas of Paris

*T*he areas situated on either side of the Seine have acquired their own character, but there is a distinction dear to the heart of Parisians between the Right Bank on the north side and the Left Bank in the south. It goes back to the Middle Ages, when the growing city started to spread along the banks of the river.

The *Rive Gauche* or Left Bank, became the students' headquarters and has since been the favourite haunt of a lively bohemian society. The Latin Quarter, St-Germain-des-Prés and Montparnasse have all been favoured by intellectuals at different times.

Meanwhile, the *Rive Droite* or Right Bank, traditionally conservative, has watched, sometimes with indulgence, sometimes with annoyance and even downright anger, the antics going on across the river. A centre of business and commerce, it prides itself on having all the major department stores and *haute couture* boutiques (see **Fashion** on pages 148–9).

Even Montmartre, at one time

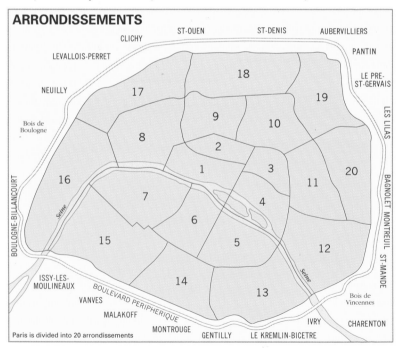

ARRONDISSEMENTS

Paris is divided into 20 arrondissements

renowned as the poor artists' quarter, has acquired a definite respectability and been overrun by tourists, while the authenticity of the red-light district of Pigalle, at the bottom of the hill, has almost disappeared.

Organising your time
You might find the following suggestions helpful when choosing a walk or an area to visit.

If you like medieval architecture and enchanting river settings, go to the Ile-de-la-Cité and the Ile St-Louis.

If you feel like taking it easy and mingling with a young crowd, aim for the Latin Quarter or St-Germain-des-Prés and watch the world go by from one of the lively cafés on the way.

If you are feeling energetic enough to take on monumental Paris, walk up the Champs Elysées or experience the thrill of admiring the city from the top of the Eiffel Tower.

If you enjoy shopping in a grand way, the Madeleine/Opéra area is the ideal choice, but if you wish to meet trendy young people, then go to Les Halles and Beaubourg.

If discreet elegance appeals to you, and you enjoy going round the art galleries, the Marais is what you are looking for.

If you like modern architecture, take the métro to La Villette or the RER to La Défense.

And if a desire for *La Bohème* compels you to go to Montmartre, ignore the artists on the place du Tertre and admire the view from the Sacré Coeur.

Coping with the weather
On a rainy day, the main cultural centres like La Villette and the Centre National

Fancy meeting you here: place St-Sulpice

d'Art et de Culture Georges Pompidou offer varied activities for all ages as well as meals and refreshments; so do large shopping centres like the Forum des Halles.

On the other hand, the department stores in the boulevard Haussmann are so close that you can go from one to the other without getting wet...and why not take the opportunity to discover one of the lovely shopping arcades near the Palais Royal, or stroll among the 250 boutiques of the Louvre des Antiquaires (see **Shopping** – see page 142).

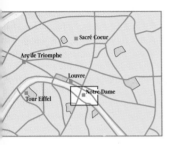

The Ile-de-la-Cité and Ile St-Louis

This is the heart of medieval Paris: the bustling Ile-de-la-Cité with Notre-Dame Cathedral solidly camped at its eastern end and, next to it, the smaller, quieter, Ile St-Louis. *Allow 2–3 hours*

Nearby:

Hôtel des Monnaies

Institut du Monde Arabe

Churches of St-Séverin and St-Julien-le-Pauvre

Place du Châtelet

Hôtel de Ville

From St-Michel métro station cross the Pont St-Michel, then turn right along the quai du Marché Neuf.

1 PLACE DU PARVIS NOTRE-DAME

Across the vast square, created by Haussmann, stands the austere Gothic cathedral that Parisians refer to, with pride and affection, simply as Notre-Dame (see page 96). Gallo-Roman and medieval remains are displayed in the Crypte Archéologique, beneath the Parvis. On the south side stands the statue of Charlemagne.

Coming out of the cathedral, turn right along the north side.

2 THE OLD CLOISTER QUARTER

The rue Chanoinesse gives a fair idea of what the area looked like in the 13th century. It was here that the canons lived and

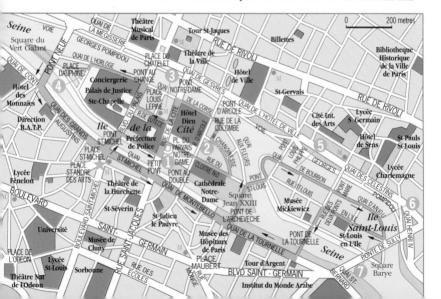

taught; original houses at nos 22 and 24 bring to mind the moving story of Héloïse and Abélard (see page 71).

Turn left along quai de la Corse then left again into rue de la Cité.

3 PLACE LOUIS-LEPINE

During the week the square is the site of a colourful flower market and on Sundays a no less picturesque but noisier bird market takes place.

Continue along rue de Lutèce. Facing are the Palais de Justice, the law courts and the Ste-Chapelle. Turn right, then left along quai de l'Horloge, past the Conciergerie, to reach place Dauphine.

4 PLACE DAUPHINE

This is a haven of peace where you might like to pause for refreshments at one of the small restaurants and admire two of the original 17th century brick and stone houses at nos 12 and 14. Beyond the statue of Henri IV, the square du Vert Galant affords beautiful views of the river.

Cross over to the Left Bank, turn left and follow the embankment, lined with bookstalls, past Notre-Dame, then cross the Pont de l'Archevêché and the Pont St-Louis and turn left.

5 QUAI DE BOURBON

In striking contrast with the feverish activity of the Cité and the Left Bank, the Ile St-Louis offers a peaceful village atmosphere, nowhere more apparent than along the cobbled quai de Bourbon lined with classical mansions. At the corner of rue des Deux Ponts, Au Franc Pinot, which has a restaurant in the vaulted cellars and a wine bar on the ground floor, is a pleasant place to stop for refreshment.

Continue along quai d'Anjou to no 17.

6 HOTEL DE LAUZUN

Built by Le Vau in 1657, the Hôtel de Lauzon had many famous occupants, including Baudelaire and Wagner, and now belongs to the City of Paris. It is well worth visiting for its interior decoration (open from Easter to November, usually at weekends).

Further on, turn right into rue St-Louis-en-l'Ile.

The incomparable cathedral of Notre-Dame

7 RUE ST-LOUIS-EN-L'ILE

This is the main street of the island. The 17th century church of St-Louis has an unusual clock outside and a richly decorated interior. A few doors away, at no 31, is the ice-cream specialist, Berthillon.

Turn left into rue des Deux Ponts, then cross the bridge. Facing you is the famous but expensive restaurant, La Tour d'Argent, and on your left the strangely modern Institut du Monde Arabe (see museums – page 92). Turn right and follow the embankment back to place St-Michel.

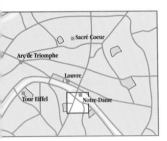

The Latin Quarter

This is the centre of university life, where tiny restaurants along the side streets and cafés on the boulevard St-Michel are packed at all hours.
Allow 2 hours (excluding visit to the Cluny Museum)

Nearby:

Jardin du

Luxembourg

Jardin des Plantes

Start from the place St-Michel, where the impressive 1860 fountain is a favourite meeting point. Take the rue de la Huchette, rue de la Harpe and rue St-Séverin to reach the church of St-Séverin (see page 57).

1 ST-SEVERIN QUARTER

The narrow streets and alleyways have kept their picturesque

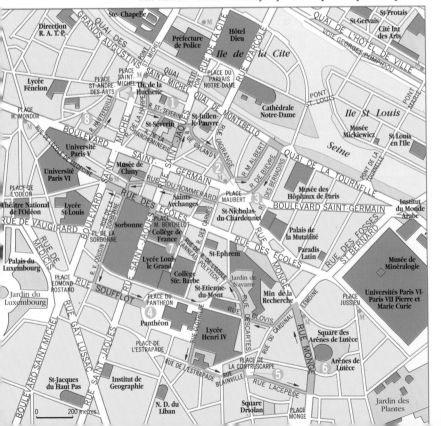

medieval names, such as 'rue de la Parcheminerie' (Parchment Street). Unfortunately, the authenticity of the district is threatened by the increasing number of cheap Greek and North African restaurants, with a welcome exception: La Cochonaille, rue de la Harpe. Le Caveau de la Huchette, rue de la Huchette, is a well-known jazz cellar.

Go round the back of St-Séverin, down the rue St-Jacques to the church of St-Julien-le-Pauvre (see page 71) and the square Viviani. Then follow the rue Galande and the rue Lagrange to the place Maubert.

2 PLACE MAUBERT

Maubert is probably a contraction of Maître Albert, the famous 13th century teacher. At one time the hide-out of thieves and cut-throats, the area has been renovated, regaining its Left Bank atmosphere. The tiny rue Maître-Albert leads down to the river from where you get a beautiful view of Notre-Dame.

Rue de Bièvre brings you back to place Maubert.

3 ST-NICOLAS-DU-CHARDONNET

Situated a little way up the rue Monge, this unusual 17th century church with a 20th-century façade, is decorated inside with paintings by Camille Corot and Charles Le Brun and elaborate funeral monuments.

Proceed along rue du Sommerard to the Musée de Cluny (see page 90), walk up rue de la Sorbonne, past the university buildings, then left into rue Soufflot.

4 PLACE DU PANTHEON

Facing you is the vast domed Panthéon dominating the whole Latin Quarter (see page 100). You can sit at one of the cafés and admire the view before going round to the left, past the bibliothèque Ste-Geneviève, famous for its ancient manuscripts.

Pass between the Panthéon and the highly original church of St-Etienne-du-Mont (see page 54) and turn right into rue Clotilde, then left into rue de l'Estrapade.

5 PLACE DE LA CONTRESCARPE

This tiny square has been famous since the Middle Ages for its cabaret de la Pomme de Pin (at no 1) described by François Rabelais, and its lively atmosphere. There is a choice of cafés and restaurants here.

Following rue Lacépède to the end leads to the Fontaine Cuvier (see page 64). However, turn left into rue Monge.

6 ARENES DE LUTECE

Rue des Arènes, on the right, leads to the ruins of a Roman theatre, discovered during the remodelling of medieval Paris in the 19th century and now part of a public garden.

Turn left at the crossroads, right into rue Descartes, then bear left down rue de Lanneau.

7 COLLEGE DE FRANCE

Since its foundation by François I in 1530, the college has maintained a tradition of independent teaching and gives free public lectures on a wide range of subjects.

Continue along rue des Ecoles past square Paul-Painlevé. Cross boulevard St-Michel.

8 RUE HAUTEFEUILLE

This old picturesque street on your right, by the former Ecole de Médecine, takes you back to place St-André-des-Arts (see page 107).

St-Germain-des-Prés

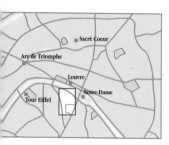

Literary cafés, jazz cellars, informal bistros, bookshops, fashion boutiques and antique shops, as well as one of the oldest churches in Paris, are the main attractions of the area. *Allow 2 hours*

Nearby:

Rue St-André-des-Arts

Rue de Buci market

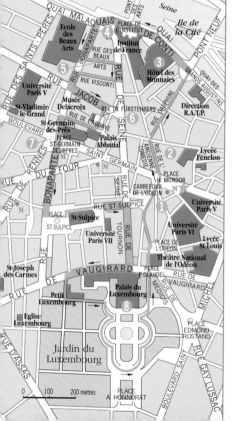

Start from the Odeon métro station.

1 CARREFOUR DE L'ODEON

Cross over the boulevard St-Germain: no 130 marks the entrance of the Cour du Commerce St-André. This alleyway and covered arcade has revolutionary associations: Marat's newspaper, *l'Ami du Peuple,* was printed at no 8 and it was here that Dr Guillotin's deadly invention was first tested on sheep! On your right is the entrance to the picturesque courtyards of the Cour de Rohan. *Retrace your steps and turn right.*

2 RUE DE L'ANCIENNE COMEDIE

The most prestigious theatre company in France, the Comédie-Française, performed at no 14 until 1770. The Café Procope opposite has, since 1686, been the meeting-place of writers, politicians and philosophers (see page 105). *Follow rue Dauphine to the embankment and turn left.*

3 HOTEL DES MONNAIES

The late-18th century building, formerly the mint, houses the Musée de la Monnaie. The displays include medals, tools, presses, engravings and drawings (open 1pm–6pm, closed Mondays, admission charge). *Continue along quai de Conti to the place de l'Institut.*

4 INSTITUT DE FRANCE

The 17th century, domed building by Le Vau houses the Bibliothèque Mazarine, which contains Cardinal Mazarin's own collection of rare books. Since 1805 it has also been the home of the Institut de France, founded during the 1789 Revolution. It includes five academies, the oldest and most famous being the Académie Française set up by Richelieu in 1635.

Turn left into rue Bonaparte; on the right is the Ecole des Beaux Arts (Academy of Art), which can be seen from the courtyard.

5 RUES DES BEAUX-ARTS, VISCONTI AND JACOB

The whole area had many famous inhabitants including Oscar Wilde, Jean Racine, Honoré de Balzac, Eugene Delacroix and Camille Corot. The rue de Seine is lined with art galleries and rue Jacob has many antique shops and a couple of quiet hotels. Near by is rue de Buci, with its well-known street market and several restaurants.

From rue Jacob turn right into rue de Fürstemberg.

6 PLACE DE FÜRSTEMBERG

This charming little square seems to belong to another time and place: it looks delightfully provincial with its romantic catalpa trees and old-fashioned street lamps. Delacroix had his studio at no 6; this is now a museum with mementoes of the artist (closed: Tuesday).

Rue de l'Abbaye brings you back to rue Bonaparte; turn left. The church of St-Germain des Prés was once part of a powerful abbey. Close by is the wide boulevard St-Germain.

7 LITERARY TRADITION

Immediately on your right is the Café des Deux Magots and, almost next door, the Café de Flore, where intellectuals and artists have been meeting for generations. It is a good spot to get the feel of the area over a cup of coffee. The Brasserie Lipp opposite is a rather more select rendezvous for celebrities.

Continue up rue Bonaparte, then turn left into rue St-Sulpice. Pass the church and turn right along rue de Tournon.

8 LUXEMBOURG

Marie de Médicis, widow of Henri IV, had the palace modelled on the Palazzo Pitti in Florence. It is now the seat of the Sénat. The gardens are adorned with numerous statues and the famous Fontaine de Médicis (see page 65).

Coming out of the gardens, follow rue Rotrou to the 18th century place de l'Odéon. Rue Crébillon and rue Condé take you back to the Carrefour de l'Odéon.

Rue de Buci: relaxing by a floral forest

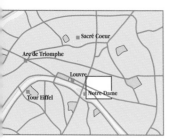

The Marais

This area of great architectural wealth is a fashionable residential district enlivened by a variety of small shops and restaurants, art galleries and craft workshops. *Allow 2 hours (excluding museum visits)*

Nearby:

Centre Pompidou

Hôtel de Sens

Village-St-Paul

The Bastille

Begin from the place St-Gervais (métro Hôtel de Ville). Facing is St-Gervais-St-Protais, the oldest classical church in Paris.

1 RUE FRANÇOIS-MIRON

This was one of the first roads to cross the marshy area or *marais*. Nos 11 and 13 are half-timbered, 15th-century houses and, almost opposite, there are splendid Gothic cellars at nos 44–46. Further up the road, the 17th-century Hôtel de

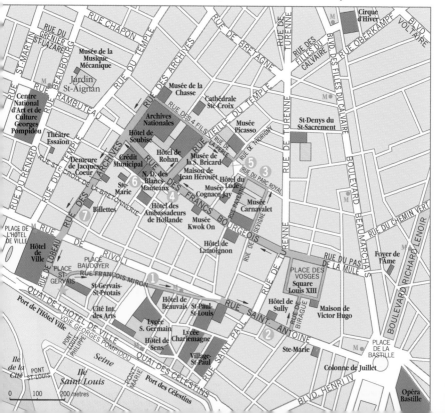

Beauvais (no 68) rang with Mozart's music when the young prodigy stayed there in 1763.

Notice the wrought-iron decorations of no 74 and the attractive balconies of the Hôtel Hénaut de Cantorbe (no 82) built in the early 18th century.
The baroque church of St-Paul-St-Louis stands at the beginning of rue Saint-Antoine.

2 RUE ST-ANTOINE
This has been the main street of the Marais since the 14th century, when it was a favourite venue for jousting contests. Henri II was fatally wounded here in 1559 when he foolishly took part in a tournament to celebrate his daughter's wedding.

The rue de Sévigné opposite the church leads to place du Marché-Ste-Catherine where you will find a good selection of restaurants. In the courtyard of the Hôtel de Sully (no 62), built in 1625, there are impressive sculptures featuring the seasons and the elements.
Turn left into rue de Birague, leading to the breathtakingly beautiful place des Vosges (see page 101). Take rue des Francs-Bourgeois going west then turn right into rue de Sévigné.

3 RUES DU PARC ROYAL AND PAYENNE
On your left is the imposing Hôtel Carnavalet which houses the Musée Historique de la Ville de Paris. Turn left at the end of the street; a row of lovely mansions facing a peaceful garden make a perfect setting. In rue Payenne, there is another garden, adorned with statues and an orangery, opposite two elegant mansions.
Turn right.

4 RUE DES FRANCS BOURGEOIS
Its medieval name, referring to the almshouses built in the 14th century for the non tax-paying citizens or _francs bourgeois,_ and the house of Jean Hérouët (no 54), with its elegant turret, recall the days when the street was the centre of the weaving trade. Today it is lined with 17th- and 18th- century mansions, pleasant little boutiques, and cafés-restaurants such as L'Orée du Marais at no 29.
Turn right into rue Vieille-du-Temple. Turn right into rue de la Perle.

5 MUSEE DE LA SERRURE
Housed in a smaller-scale mansion, once the home of the architect who built Les Invalides, the museum's collection traces the history of locks since Roman times (closed: Sunday, Monday and August).
Rue de Thorigny opposite leads to the Musée Picasso (see page 94). Turn back down rue de la Perle and walk along rue des 4 Fils; on the right is the Musée de la Chasse et de la Nature (see page 79); turn left into rue des Archives then left again into rue des Francs Bourgeois, past the beautiful Hôtel de Soubise.

6 NOTRE-DAME-DES-BLANCS-MANTEAUX
This church is famous for its woodwork, in particular its rococo pulpit and organ loft. Concerts are given here during the Marais festival.
Return to the rue des Archives and turn left.

7 CLOITRE DES BILLETTES
Built in the 14th century as part of a monastery, this is the only medieval cloister left in Paris. The church next door is 18th-century.

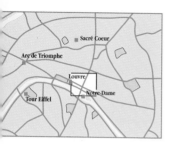

Beaubourg and Les Halles

Major redevelopment gave this district a new lease of life in the 1970s, and today the area attracts a crowd of young trend-setters, while the gastronomic tradition has been maintained by the score of small restaurants that used to surround the old food market. *Allow 2 hours (excluding visit to Georges Pompidou Centre)*

Coming out of the Hôtel de Ville métro station, follow avenue Victoria and turn right into rue St-Martin.

Nearby:

Louvre Museum

Théâtre de la Ville

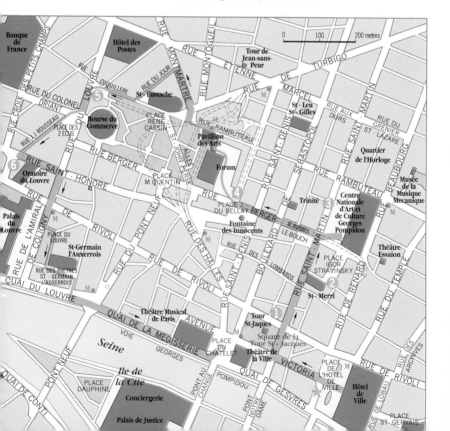

1 TOUR ST-JACQUES

The Tour St-Jacques on the left is all that remains of the 16th-century church of St-Jacques-de-la-Boucherie, a starting-point for pilgrims bound for Santiago de Compostela. Near by there is a statue of Pascal, who conducted barometric experiments in the tower. *Continue along rue St-Martin.*

2 AROUND ST-MERRI

The names of the streets surrounding the late Gothic church of St-Merri recall their association with medieval trades. There is rue de la Verrerie (glass-makers) alongside the church and, opposite, rue des Lombards, who set themselves up as moneylenders. The rue St-Martin is lined with shops and bistros. On the north side of the church, the intrusion of the 20th century is emphasised by the colourful fountain in the middle of the place Igor-Stravinsky. *Just north of the place is the Centre Georges Pompidou*

3 CENTRE POMPIDOU

Although used to designate the Centre Pompidou, Beaubourg is, in fact, the name of the old district that, after years of neglect, has suddenly come into the limelight following the success of the cultural centre (see page 52). The noisy animation of the Piazza in front of it will draw your immediate attention, as street entertainers provide a permanent show. North of the Centre lies the Quartier de l'Horloge: a lively pedestrian area made up of narrow streets and arcades, with numerous shops and a curious modern clock, called Le Défenseur du Temps (the Defender of Time), in rue Bernard-de-Clairvaux. *Return to the Piazza and turn right into the rue Aubry-le-Boucher.*

4 LES HALLES

Rest a while in the square des Innocents: it has the most beautiful Renaissance fountain in the middle. The neat gardens that have replaced the old food market give the area an air of tranquillity, but do not be misled by appearances: the hubbub that was typical of Les Halles has simply gone underground! Escalators lead down into the Forum, a multi-level entertainment and shopping centre (see page 66). *Come up on the rue Rambuteau side and walk to the church of St-Eustache (see page 54), then round it for the best views.*

5 BOURSE DU COMMERCE

As you leave rue du Jour, you can see the Bourse du Commerce in front of you; it replaced the city's corn exchange in 1889. To the right is rue Coquillère lined with restaurants, including the famous *Au Pied de Cochon.* Half-way down rue Jean-Jacques-Rousseau on the right is the charming Galerie Véro-Dodat with its quaint shops. *At the end of the street, turn left into rue St-Honoré.*

6 ORATOIRE DU LOUVRE

The 17th-century church by Le Mercier was used as the royal chapel under Louis XIII, Louis XIV and Louis XV, who listened to the sermons of famous preachers such as Bossuet. After the revolution of 1789, it became a Protestant church. *Turn right into rue du Louvre to reach the embankment; the church of St-Germain-l'Auxerrois (see page 55) offers an interesting mixture of styles. Admire the lovely view of the Conciergerie from the quai de la Mégisserie. The place du Châtelet, where you can take the métro, has an impressive fountain in the middle.*

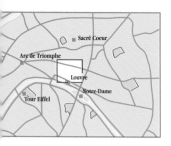

From the Opéra to the Palais-Royal

The prestigious Opéra House and the elegant Palais-Royal epitomise the impression of refinement and grandeur that one gets from this walk. *Allow 2 hours*

Nearby:

Musée Grévin

Madeleine

Louvre Museum

Jardin des Tuileries

Begin from the place de l'Opéra (métro Opéra). Cross the boulevard des Capucines then turn right.

1 RUE DE LA PAIX

Named rue Napoléon when it was opened in 1806, it is today lined with expensive jewellers (the famous Cartier is at no 11) and has become the symbol of luxury. It leads into the no-less-

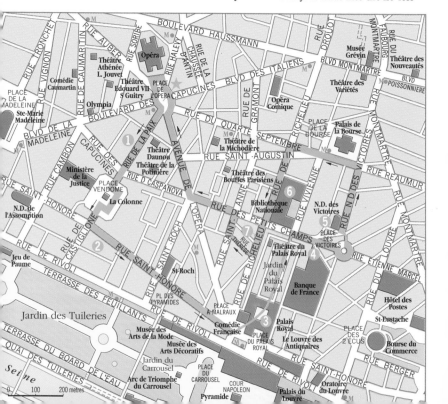

elegant and harmonious place Vendôme, which Napoleon admires from the top of the central column.
Cross the square, walk along rue de Castiglione and turn left.

2 RUE ST-HONORE

The Carré des Feuillants on the corner of the rue de Castiglione is a fashionable but expensive restaurant where you can experiment with *la nouvelle cuisine*. The church of St-Roch halfway down the street stood on a hillock known as the Butte Saint-Roch. The hillock was completely levelled for the building of the avenue de l'Opéra: before that, you had to go down seven steps to gain access to the church, whereas now you have to go up 13! Further along the street on the right, rue des Pyramides leads to the square which bears the same name with a gilded statue of Joan of Arc, erected in the 19th century on the very spot where she was wounded during an attempt to deliver Paris from English occupation.
Follow rue St-Honoré which leads to the Palais-Royal.

3 PALAIS-ROYAL

As you reach the place André-Malraux, you get a splendid view of the Opéra to your left.

Across the square is the Théâtre-Français, home of the famous Comédie-Française (see page 98). Close by is place Colette, from where you enter the Palais-Royal gardens. Before you do, however, carry on a little further to the Louvre des Antiquaires, which has 250 shops and a convenient restaurant.
Walk through the Jardin du Palais-Royal. Turn right into rue des Petits-Champs and, if you are ready for a meal, try the Mercure Galant at no 15.

4 GALERIES COLBERT AND VIVIENNE

These charming covered arcades date from the early 19th century; the Galerie Vivienne is the most beautiful of the two with its carved, vaulted ceiling and glass roof, its old-fashioned bookshop and tea room.
Rue des Petits-Champs leads to the circular place des Victoires with a statue of Louis XIV in the centre (see page 107). Leave by rue Vide-Gousset.

5 NOTRE-DAME-DES-VICTOIRES

The 17th-century church is famous for its seven paintings by Van Loo, its fine monument to the composer Lully, its beautiful organ and more than 30,000 ex-votos covering the walls.
Continue along rue Notre-Dame-des-Victoires, turn left past the Palais de la Bourse (the Stock Exchange), then left again into rue de Richelieu

6 BIBLIOTHEQUE NATIONALE

France's national library is due to be transferred to new premises in the 13th *arrondissement* and renamed the Bibliothèque de France. Originally based on royal collections, it now houses more than 12 million printed books and as many engravings.

7 FONTAINE MOLIERE

Further along rue de Richelieu, you will see a 19th-century fountain, dedicated to Molière, not far from the house (now no 40) where he died in 1673 after collapsing on stage (see page 65).
Turn right into rue Thérèse then follow rue Ste-Anne back to rue des Petits-Champs; on the corner stands Lully's house adorned with musical motifs. Walk back along avenue de l'Opéra.

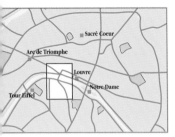

Rive Droite, Rive Gauche

This walk takes you from the 'royal' Tuileries Gardens across the river to the Faubourg St-Germain, once fashionable with the aristocracy whose splendid mansions have now been taken over by ministries and embassies. *Allow 2 hours (excluding visit to Musée d'Orsay)*

Nearby:

Rue du Faubourg-
St-Honoré
Place Vendôme
Invalides
Pont Alexandre III

Begin from the Concorde métro station.

1 RUE DE RIVOLI

The elegant arcades used to be lined with smart shops but these are now being replaced by souvenir shops. There are still a few luxury hotels such as the Meurice at no 228, head-quarters of the German high command during World War II. *Enter the Tuileries Gardens on your right.*

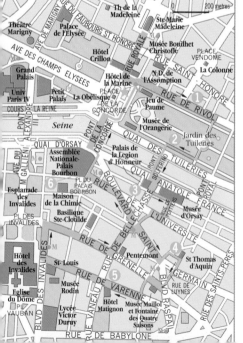

2 JARDIN DES TUILERIES

Laid in 1664 by Louis XIV's chief gardener, André Le Nôtre, the gardens soon became a popular place for strolling. The western end is quite elaborate with its octagonal pool surrounded by statues, terraces and twin pavilions while, from the round pool at the other end, the view extends all the way up the Champs-Elysées to the Arc de Triomphe.

The Terrasse du Bord de l'Eau, by the river, affords good views of the Left Bank. Cross the Pont de Solferino.

3 PALAIS DE LA LEGION D'HONNEUR

Take rue de Bellechasse between the impressive new Musée d'Orsay (left), which has a convenient restaurant, and the Musée de la Légion d'Honneur (right) which illustrates the history of

The Tuileries' Jeu de Paume for modern art

the orders of French Chivalry before the 1789 Revolution and of the Legion of Honour founded by Napoleon in 1802 (closed: Monday)
Turn left into rue de Lille. Rue de Poitiers leads into rue de l'Université. On reaching the boulevard St-Germain, turn left, then left again into rue du Bac.

4 ST-THOMAS D'AQUIN
Begun in the 17th century and finished in the 18th, this church, on the right, was originally the chapel of a Dominican monastery. Inside are some fine 17th- and 18th-century paintings, which provide a perfect setting for the regular Sunday organ concerts.
Follow rue de Luynes to rue de Grenelle and turn right past the elaborate Fontaine des Quatre Saisons (see page 65), then left.

5 RUE DE VARENNE
The name of the street is derived from *garenne* (warren), a reminder of the days when the Faubourg was a rural area. It is lined with several stately mansions: the most famous is the Hôtel Matignon at no 57, the Prime Minister's official residence since 1958. Built in 1721 and

once owned by Talleyrand, it has the largest private gardens in Paris. Its contemporary, the Hôtel Biron at the end of the street also has beautiful gardens. It houses a museum dedicated to the sculptor Rodin who lived there.
Turn right, then right again into rue de Grenelle, taking a look at the smaller scale Hôtel de Villars at no 118.

6 PALAIS BOURBON
The rue de Bellechasse and the boulevard St-Germain bring you back to the river, past the impressive Palais Bourbon (seat of the Assemblée Nationale), remodelled by Napoleon to match the Madeleine facing it on the other side of the place de la Concorde.
Cross the Pont de la Concorde and the place de la Concorde, then follow rue Royale towards the Madeleine.

View Impressionism at the Musée d'Orsay

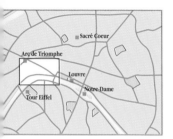

The Champs Elysées

This symbol of French elegance and glamour offers a unique and thrilling view that sweeps uphill to the Arc de Triomphe. *Allow 2 hours*

Nearby:

Tuileries Gardens

Musée de l'Orangerie

Madeleine

Musée Jacquemart-André

Avenue Montaigne,

Palais de Tokyo

Musée Guimet

Théâtre de Champs Elysées

Start from place de la Concorde (métro Concorde).

1 CHAMPS ELYSEES

The avenue was designed in the 17th century as a royal way leading out of Paris towards Versailles. Later, it became extremely fashionable to be seen driving along it in a horse-drawn carriage. In recent years, the Champs Elysées has been the scene of all major national celebrations, such as the bicentenary of the 1789 Revolution and, of course, the march past on 14 July.
Start walking along the main avenue.

2 CONCORDE TO THE ROND-POINT

The paved avenue is lined on both sides with green open spaces planted with chestnut trees after the English fashion, the romantic alleys leading to half-concealed pavilions such as those occupied by the American Embassy and the Espace Cardin on the right-hand side.
Walk through the gardens on the left, and turn right along the Cours La Reine then right again into avenue Winston Churchill.

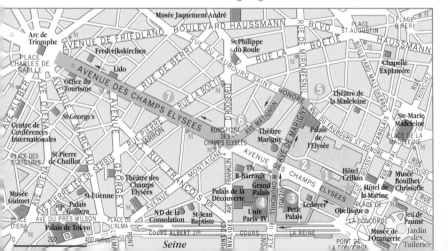

Tomb of the Unknown Soldier, Arc de Triomphe

3 PETIT PALAIS

Like the Grand Palais facing it, the Petit Palais was built of stone and steel for the 1900 Exposition Universelle and now houses the art collections of the city of Paris: Greek, Roman and Egyptian art, medieval and Renaissance objects, books and enamels, 16th- and 17th-century Dutch and Flemish paintings, 18th-century furniture and tapestries and 19th-century French paintings by Courbet, Delacroix, Cézanne, etc (closed: Monday).

4 GRAND PALAIS

In this imposing, glass-roofed building, adorned with an Ionic colonnade and elaborate sculptures, major art exhibitions are traditionally held and the long queues winding outside this temple of culture are a familiar sight. At the back is the Palais de la Découverte, once a very popular science museum, but now overshadowed by the ultra-modern Cité des Sciences at La Villette.

Cross the Champs Elysées and continue along avenue de Marigny.

5 PALAIS DE L'ELYSEE

On your left, at the corner of the avenue Gabriel, a stamp market is held on Thursdays and Sundays. Further along on the right, is the Palais de l'Elysée, built in 1718 and counting among its famous owners the Marquise de Pompadour and Napoleon's sister Caroline. Since 1873 it has been the official residence of the Président de la République.

Turn left into rue du Faubourg-St-Honoré, lined with shops, then left again into avenue Matignon .

6 ROND-POINT DES CHAMPS-ELYSEES

Designed by Le Nôtre, it has an array of beautiful flowerbeds and fountains; several of the surrounding buildings, such as the Théâtre Renaud-Barrault, date from the 19th century (its restaurant would provide a pleasant break at this point).

Continue up the Champs Elysées.

7 ROND-POINT TO THE ARC DE TRIOMPHE

This section offers a marked contrast with the more pastoral lower section. Of the fashionable mansions built around 1860, only one has survived, no 25. It belonged to La Païva, an adventuress whose receptions were attended by writers and artists. The wide pavements are continually teeming with a colourful cosmopolitan crowd attracted by the shopping arcades, cafés, restaurants, cinemas and big stores like Virgin Megastore. On the quieter, south side is Fouquet's Restaurant, where celebrities come to be seen.

From the Trocadero to the Invalides

This is the Paris of grand vistas and wide open spaces, where various architectural styles help to create an impressive setting for the most famous of the city's monuments, the Eiffel Tower. *Allow 2–3 hours (excluding museum visits and a climb to the top of the Eiffel Tower)*

Begin from the Trocadero métro station.

1 PLACE DU TROCADERO

From the top of the Chaillot hill, the rather dull place du Trocadero offers stunning views of the Left Bank. Several wide avenues radiating from it give the impression of a busy roundabout where no one cares to stop. Behind a high wall to the west is the Passy cemetery and, facing the river, the Palais

Nearby :

Left Bank – antique shops of the Village Suisse

Musée Rodin

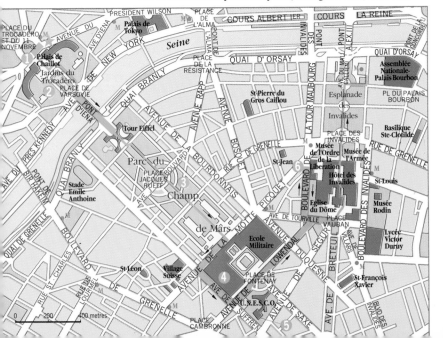

de Chaillot built for the 1937 Exposition Universelle. The name Trocadero commemorates the capture in 1823 of Fort Trocadero in Spain.
Pass between the curved wings of the Palais de Chaillot.

2 JARDINS DU TROCADERO

Stairs lead down to the gardens on either side of a long pool adorned with stone and gilt bronze statues and attractive floodlit fountains, which provide one of the most spectacular summer night shows of the capital.
Cross the Pont d'Iéna, named to commemorate Napoleon's victory over the Prussians in 1806. The bridge provides a good close-up view of the Eiffel Tower.

3 CHAMP DE MARS

If, after the thrill of climbing up to the third floor of the Eiffel Tower, you feel the need to relax in a down-to-earth restaurant, a rare thing in this rather select district, then la Fontaine de Mars, 129 rue St-Dominique, is just what you are looking for.

The vast open space, stretching from the Eiffel Tower to the Ecole Militaire, was originally designed in the 18th century as a parade-ground for the nearby military academy, hence its name. Later on, it became the tradition to use it for large-scale public festivals and World Exhibitions; thus, in 1989, almost half a million people attended the mammoth celebrations for the 100th birthday of the Eiffel Tower.
Walk across the park and turn right into avenue de la Motte Picquet.

4 ECOLE MILITAIRE

The building of this magnificent neoclassical Military Academy, designed by Louis XV's architect, Jacques-Ange Gabriel, was actually financed by a special tax on playing-cards.

Napoleon Bonaparte was undoubtedly its most famous cadet, passing out as a lieutenant in the artillery with the comment: 'Will go far, given favourable circumstances'. The school is still used as an instruction centre and is closed to the public.
As you walk round the building, you might enjoy a short detour to the antique shops of the Village Suisse across the avenue de Suffren.

5 UNESCO BUILDING

Inaugurated in 1958, this home of the United Nations Educational, Scientific and Cultural Organisation is the result of close international co-operation: three architects, an American, an Italian and a Frenchman were responsible for the project, while the decoration was left to such famous artists as Henry Moore (monumental sculpture), Alexander Calder (mobile), Pablo Picasso (mural), Joán Miró (ceramics), Lurçat and Le Corbusier (tapestries) and Isamu Noguchi (fountain).
Follow avenue de Lowendal and walk to no 51bis, boulevard de La Tour Maubourg.

6 MUSEE DE L'ORDRE DE LA LIBERATION

The order, created by General de Gaulle in 1940, is the highest honour bestowed by France in recognition of outstanding services rendered during World War II. Among the allied leaders honoured are: King George VI, Winston Churchill and General Eisenhower (closed: Sunday).
Retrace your steps and turn left. Go through the Hôtel des Invalides (see page 68) and walk across the Esplanade to the Invalides métro station.

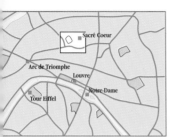

Montmartre

Although it remains a symbol of bohemian life, *La Butte,* as Parisians call it, has lost some of its romantic appeal. There are times, however, when walking along the quaint old streets takes you back a hundred years! *Allow 2 hours*

Begin from the Pigalle métro station.

Nearby:

Montmartre cemetery

Musée d'Art Juif

Musée d'Art Naif

Max Fournay

1 PIGALLE

For 100 years the name has been associated with a kind of exuberant and colourful night-life, usually summed up in two words: Moulin Rouge!

That famous institution is still as popular as ever, but the area has now been taken over by less picturesque clubs, discos, sex-shops and pornographic cinemas. It is not advisable for women to walk round Pigalle at night on their own.

Walk along boulevard de Rochechouart, and turn left into rue de Steinkerque.

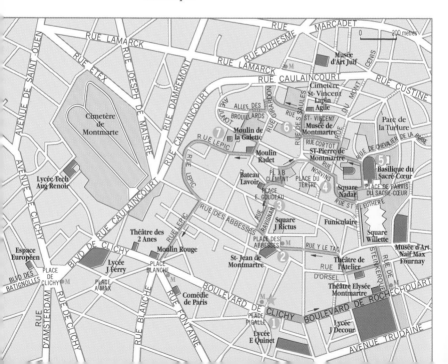

2 PLACE DES ABBESSES

At the end of the street, a funicular leads directly to the Sacré-Coeur Basilica. Turn left into rue Tardieu and continue along the rue Yvonne-Le-Tac: a chapel stands on the site where it is thought Saint-Denis was martyred in the third century. Notice the métro entrance on the place des Abbesses, with its glass-roofed, wrought-iron structure, originally designed by Hector Guimard at the turn of the century. St-Jean l'Evangéliste, dating from the same period, was the first church to be built of concrete.

Leave by rue des Abbesses and turn right into the twisting rue Ravignan.

3 PLACE EMILE-GOUDEAU

On this charming square, complete with fountain, you can see a reconstruction of the Bateau-Lavoir, burnt down in 1970, where Picasso and friends made history (see page 83).

Continue to the end of rue Ravignan. Follow rue Norvins.

4 PLACE DU TERTRE

Entirely focused on the tourist trade, this old village square has lost its authenticity but you can just about imagine what it was like in the 1920s. The tiny place du Calvaire in the southwest corner offers exceptional views of the capital.

Leave place du Tertre past the old church of St-Pierre (see page 81) and walk to the Sacré-Coeur Basilica.

5 SACRE-COEUR

If you don't mind crowds, you will enjoy the majesty of the place and the vast panorama in front. The back streets are quieter and you may wish to have a meal in the appropriately named, local restaurant: Atmosphère, 18 rue du Chevalier-de-la-Barre.

Walk across rue du Mont-Cenis and along rue Cortot where no 12 houses the Musée de Montmartre (see page 81). Turn right at the end of the street.

Sacre-Coeur, atop Paris' highest point

6 RUE DES SAULES

This is one of the most picturesque streets, running downhill from the Butte. On the right is the Montmartre vineyard and, on the other side of rue Saint-Vincent, the Lapin Agile, which has hardly changed since the days of Picasso and Vlaminck. In the Cimetière St-Vincent opposite, you can see Utrillo's grave.

Walk along rue St-Vincent and turn left up some stairs to the Château des Brouillards, an 18th-century folly. Beyond is avenue Junot; turn left then right into rue Lepic.

7 MOULIN DE LA GALETTE

The old mill on your right was once a famous dance hall painted by Renoir and Van Gogh, who lived with his brother at no 54.

Follow the street to the bottom of the hill. On the corner stands the Moulin Rouge.

Arc de Triomphe

*T*he Arc de Triomphe has, like the Eiffel Tower, a magnetic appeal for visitors from all over the world. This can, to a large extent, be explained by its exceptional situation at the top of a hill, almost halfway between the Louvre and La Défense. Its square outline, easily spotted from afar, is well defined against the sky by day and illuminated by night.

Thirty years to build...

Commissioned in 1806 by Napoleon as a tribute to his Grande Armée, it is the largest triumphal arch ever built in the pure tradition of Roman architecture. The design was that of architect Jean Chalgrin. However, work progressed slowly (it took two years to lay the foundations!). Chalgrin died in 1811 and the construction of the arch almost came to a halt after the fall of Napoleon. It was finally completed in 1836.

The arch today

In 1840, the hearse carrying Napoleon's remains quite appropriately passed under the arch on its way to Les Invalides. Then, in 1920, the Unknown Soldier was buried beneath it, under a plain slab and, since 11 November 1923, a remembrance ceremony has been held every year. The flame is rekindled every evening at 6.30pm. On special occasions, a huge flag floats beneath the arch to splendid effect.

Viewed from a distance

The arch is 50m high, 45m wide and 22m thick. Of the four massive sculptures carved in high relief on the façades, only the one by François Rude has become famous for its bold inspiration. Known as *La Marseillaise*, it depicts the departure in 1792 of the volunteers, spurred on by a winged figure representing France. Smaller reliefs on the façades and the sides feature various victories won during the 1789 Revolution and the First Empire; a frieze by Rude and five other sculptors runs all the way round the arch. Along the top there is a row of shields inscribed with the names of victories won by Napoleon's Grande Armée.

A closer view

A subway leads from the northern pavement of the Champs Elysées to the

GLORIOUS AND SOMBRE MOMENTS

In 1885, Victor Hugo, France's most popular man of letters, lay in state beneath the arch before being buried in the Panthéon. On 14 July 1919, the allied armies celebrated their victory by marching through the arch. In 1940, the German army marched triumphantly past it greeted only by deadly silence. In 1944, General de Gaulle was given a riotous welcome by the people of Paris, and on 14 July 1989, the arch was the focal point of the celebrations for the bicentenary of the 1789 Revolution.

Place Charles-de-Gaulle, 75008. Tel: 43 80 31 31. Platform and museum open: 10am–5pm. Admission charge. Métro Charles-de-Gaulle-Etoile. Access by subway from the north side of the Champs-Elysées.

Nearby:

Flower market on place des Ternes FNAC hi-fi centre in avenue des Ternes Shopping arcades along the Champs Elysées.

The Arc de Triomphe by night

base of the arch. Underneath, the names of hundreds of generals are inscribed on the walls: those who died in action are underlined. It is worth climbing to the platform on top of the arch by means of the lift or stairs. The perfectly symmetrical place de l'Etoile and the 12 avenues radiating from it offer a stunning view.

To the west is the vast modern complex of La Défense. The small museum houses an exhibition explaining the construction of the arch and the main events connected with it; there is a video in French and English.

The place Charles-de-Gaulle

It used to be called place de l'Etoile because of its star shape, until it was renamed after General de Gaulle's death; but tradition dies hard and l'Etoile it remains in the heart of all Parisians. Over 100 years ago, Haussmann remodelled it and built elegant neoclassical mansions all round. The 120m-wide avenue Foch is the most exclusive residential street in Paris; among its illustrious inhabitants were the Duke and Duchess of Windsor.

Bastille

*E*ven though all traces of the gruesome past disappeared long ago, the name Bastille is still charged with significance. In the minds of French people it has remained a symbol of the fight for freedom, celebrated every year on 14 July.

The Bastille fortress

Built in the 14th century as part of new fortifications to extend the city on the Right Bank, it was also intended as a residence for Charles V, who felt better protected from eventual uprisings away from the city centre. During the reign of Louis XIII it became the hated state prison and symbol of oppression that was the focus of the people's anger in 1789.

The Bastille held some famous prisoners, including the Man in the Iron Mask, presumed to be Louis XIV's twin brother, the finance minister, Fouquet, and the philosopher, Voltaire. Shortly before the revolution the prison was partially cleared and held only seven prisoners when the mob took it by storm on 14 July 1789. However, its fall unleashed the spirit of freedom throughout France.

Demolition began almost immediately. Some of the stones were used for the construction of the Pont de la Concorde, and within a year there was no trace of the massive fortress. On the first anniversary of the fall of the Bastille, people danced on the site.

The place de la Bastille

The central column, called the Colonne de Juillet (July Column), commemorates the Parisians who died during the July 1830 Revolution. This lasted only three days, *les Trois Glorieuses;* the victims were buried underneath the monument and their names carved on the shaft. At the top of the 50m high column stands the elf-like figure of the *Génie de la Liberté,* the Spirit of Liberty. Paving stones follow the outline of the Bastille fortress on this otherwise ordinary square, a traditional meeting-place for demonstrations and celebrations.

The Opéra Bastille

In 1989, the fate of the whole district took a different turn with the opening of Paris's second opera house, which had already become a controversial issue in various Parisian circles. The intention behind the project was to provide the capital with an opera house that was better adapted technically to modern productions, while creating a new artistic centre in the less favoured eastern part of Paris. The Opéra Bastille, built by the young Canadian architect, Carlos Ott, was inaugurated on 13 July 1989, as a preamble to the celebrations for the bicentenary of the French Revolution

In stark contrast to the ornate Opéra Garnier, the gently curved, sober façade of the building catches the faintest ray of sunlight, thus brightening up the surrounding area.

The Bastille district

Traditionally occupied by craftsmen and small shopkeepers, the district surrounding the place de la Bastille had,

Place de Bastille: a bustling crossroads where a prison once stood

by the end of the 1970s, become generally run-down, even derelict in parts. It is undergoing complete renovation and looks like becoming as chic and sought-after as its neighbour the Marais. Art galleries, bars and fashionable nightclubs are to be found next to old-fashioned shops and dilapidated houses. The most colourful and liveliest streets are the rue de la Roquette and the rue de Lappe to the north of the square.

The Pavillon de l'Arsenal

Between the place de la Bastille and the Seine is the Port de Plaisance de Paris Arsenal, a new marina that helps to smarten up the area. To the southwest, at the end of the boulevard Henri IV, a very interesting new museum has recently opened, the Pavillon de l'Arsenal. It illustrates architecture and town planning in Paris through the ages and explains current and future developments.

Opéra Bastille, place de la Bastille, 75012. Tel: 40 01 19 70 for information on guided tours. Admission charge. Métro Bastille.

Pavillon de l'Arsenal, 21 boulevard Morland, 75004.

Tel: 42 76 33 97. Open weekdays: 10.30am–6.00pm, Sunday 11am–7pm. Closed: Monday. Métro Sully-Morland.

Nearby:

The Marais

Ile-St-Louis.

Revolutionary Paris

Ever since Paris was granted independent status in the 13th century, Parisians have never hesitated to rise against excessive political power and the city has come to be considered as a very sensitive barometer of discontent.

The first major dual between the monarchy and the French people was fought and won in Paris in 1789. The signal was given when the crowd swept along the Faubourg St-Antoine to bring down the mighty Bastille. As a symbolic gesture, the Pont de la Concorde was later completed with stones from the hated prison, so that 'the people could for ever trample the ruins of the old fortress'. Time and again, Parisians took the initiative, marching on Versailles to ask the king for bread, charging the Tuileries guards, listening to their leaders' fiery speeches in the Palais-Royal gardens, watching with gruesome curiosity as the rickety carts full of condemned prisoners jolted along the streets to the place of execution, or simply dancing and rejoicing on the Champ de Mars on the first anniversary of Bastille Day. Scenes like these are vividly described in Dickens's *Tale of Two Cities*.

During the 19th century, the streets of Paris were set ablaze on several occasions by fierce fighting across barricades hurriedly erected from paving stones, metal grids and old mattresses. With the 1848 uprising, which began in the boulevard des Capucines, Paris did away with the monarchy for good. Yet in 1870, the Commune of Paris again challenged the government in a bitter contest that ended in bloodshed in the Père-Lachaise cemetery. This time the Parisians lost.

Images: Marie-
Antionette's
execution on Place
de la Concorde;
Louis XVI as
prisoner; the
storming of the
Bastille

A hundred years later, they
showed that tradition could easily
be revived when, in May 1968,
students and workers put up
barricades in the streets, bringing
about General de Gaulle's
resignation.

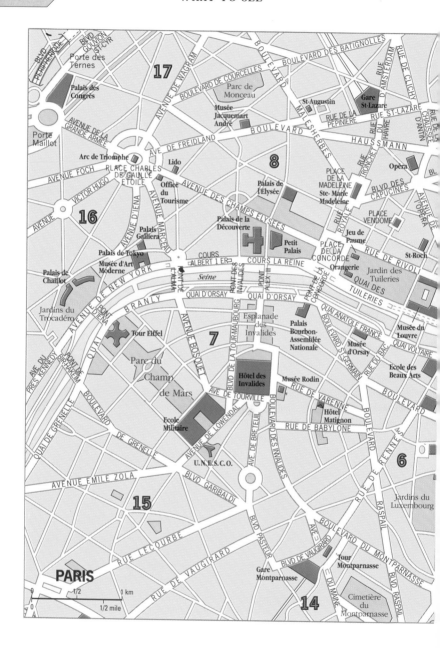

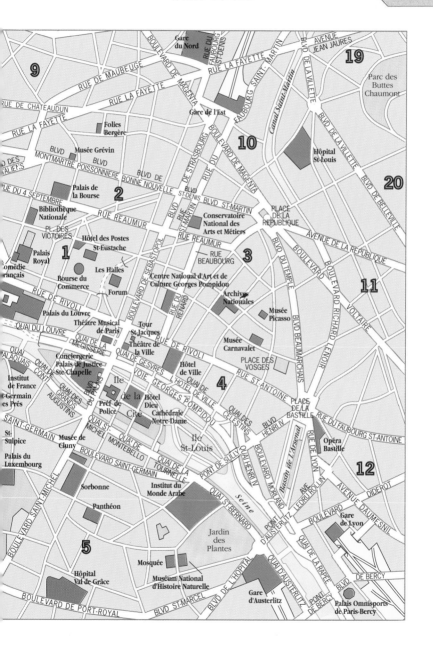

Bridges

*T*hirty bridges of greatly varying styles span the River Seine within the boulevard périphérique. Vital links between Left and Right banks, they open up large vistas across the city, thus directly contributing to its unity. Although some of them may have been rebuilt several times, their names often recall customs or events during various periods of the capital's history.

Petit-Pont, at the Seine's narrowest point

THE CITE BRIDGES
The Petit-Pont and the Pont Notre-Dame

In Roman times these were the only bridges crossing the river via the Ile-de-la-Cité; the Petit-Pont, which gets its name from being the smaller of the two, was first built of stone when the construction of Notre-Dame was undertaken, but periodic floods have taken their toll and it has been rebuilt 11 times. The present bridge dates from 1853. The Pont Notre-Dame, overladen with richly decorated houses, fell down and also had to be rebuilt several times. The latest version dates from 1913.
Métro St-Michel or Cité.

The Pont au Change

Although built during the Second Empire, this bridge has retained its medieval name, a reminder that nearly all the houses and shops built on it belonged to money-changers, who enjoyed a lucrative monopoly.
Métro Châtelet.

The Pont au Double

This bridge, linking the Left Bank and the island, acquired its strange name in the Middle Ages because the toll imposed was a coin named a *double*.
Métro St-Michel.

The Pont-Neuf

Curiously enough, this is the oldest bridge in Paris, built in the 16th century. Situated at the tip of the Ile-de-la-Cité, it offers exceptional views down river. It was never built on, a great novelty at the time, but the carvings that decorate it illustrate 'dentists' busily pulling teeth, entertainers, and assorted stalls, which were all part of the daily scene 400 years ago. The two halves, which are not in line, are separated by the place du Pont-Neuf, where there is an equestrian statue of King Henri IV.

Although it has been restored many times, the bridge remains unchanged to this day.
Métro Pont-Neuf.

The Pont Alexandre III

Built for the 1900 Exposition Universelle, this bridge provides a link between the stately classical architecture of Les Invalides and the splendidly pompous steel and glass style of the Grand Palais. Each end is adorned with two allegorical sculptures, featuring medieval France and modern France on the Left Bank side, Renaissance France and France under Louis XIV on the Right Bank side. *Métro Invalides.*

The Pont de l'Alma

The bridge dating from the Second Empire and commemorating a Franco-British victory during the Crimean War had to be replaced 20 years ago. However, the Zouave soldier beneath it was preserved. Every time the level of the Seine rose, he was partially drowned – a sure way of telling the height of the water. *Métro Alma-Marceau.*

Gleam of gilt on the Pont Alexandre III

The Pont Neuf, with 12 varying arches

The Pont des Arts

The city's first pedestrian iron bridge is a romantic structure originally dating from 1803. It is a popular place for strolling and admiring the breathtaking view of the Ile-de-la-Cité. *Métro Pont-Neuf.*

The Pont de la Concorde

Its construction was started in 1788 by the civil engineer, Jean Rodolphe Perronnet, but only completed after the fall of the Bastille. Since then, it has reflected many political upheavals by changing its name every time. However, in 1830, the name Concorde was definitely adopted (see page 35).

The Pont-Royal

Seen from the Left Bank, with the Louvre in the background, this bridge epitomises the discreet elegance that is one of the most attractive features of Paris. Its royal name is a reminder that it was built during the reign of Louis XIV by Jacques Gabriel. *Métro Rue du Bac.*

Centre Georges Pompidou

*I*ts full name – Centre National d'Art et de Culture Georges Pompidou – gives a fair idea of the vast scope of this multi-purpose cultural centre and explains its enormous popularity, in spite of the controversy that is still going on about its design 15 years after its inauguration.

BEAUBOURG

After the removal of the old food market in 1968, the Beaubourg area was included in the huge town-planning programme centred round Les Halles; President Pompidou then decided to build a multi-purpose centre for modern and contemporary art on the site.

A futuristic design

Two young architects, Richard Rogers (British) and Renzo Piano (Italian) designed the complex, which was inaugurated in 1977, three years after President Pompidou's death. To some people it looks like an oil refinery or even scaffolding on a building site, while others, with a more optimistic outlook, see it as a contemporary piece of sculpture. In order to have as much free space as possible inside, lifts, stairs, escalators and ventilation shafts were fitted on the outside, hence its cluttered appearance.

There is a public information library with French and foreign books, slides and films; an industrial design centre featuring architecture, town planning and industrial design; an acoustics and music research centre for the purpose of sound experimentation; a children's workshop; a cinema; an assortment of rooms for temporary exhibitions, concerts and lectures; and, of course, the Musée National d'Art Moderne.

Clear to all, an exterior escalator

A *laissez-passer d'une journée* (day pass) will enable you to see all the exhibitions and to visit the museum.

THE MUSEE NATIONAL D'ART MODERNE

This is situated on the third and fourth floors; the entrance is on the fourth floor, which you can reach via the serpent-like escalator accessible from the main hall.

The collections of the former Musée d'Art Moderne, retracing the evolution of art through the 20th century, were transferred from the Palais de Tokyo and have since been considerably extended to include contemporary art.

The third floor houses frequently renewed exhibits of abstract and figurative contemporary art from 1965 onwards, while the fourth floor displays all the major currents of modern art from 1905 to 1965. On this floor there are two main sections: on the south (St-Merri) side as you enter, you can see the early 20th-century trends – Fauvism and Cubism – while on the north side the main post-World-War-I trends are represented.

The south side

The striking colours characteristic of Fauvism are illustrated in works by Derain, Vlaminck and above all Matisse, while Bonnard, whose work does not fit into the main trends, is also well represented.

There is a large selection of works by the main exponents of Cubism: Braque, Picasso, Gris and also Léger.

The north side

Abstract art is represented by Mondrian, Kupka, Klee and Delaunay. The sombre, mystic style of Rouault and Chagall's world of fantasy dominate the 1920s and 30s beside the Dada movement which deliberately derided society.

Surrealism is well represented by Dali, Magritte, Ernst, Miro and Masson; so is the Cobra Group headed by Asger Jorn after World War II. The American school of Abstract Expressionism is strikingly represented by Pollock's 'drip-and-splash' style. The 1960s saw the advent of New Realism and Pop Art flourished with Andy Warhol.

The fifth floor offers you a chance to relax in the pleasant cafeteria and enjoy beautiful views over the capital.

Pompidou Centre: something for everyone

75191 Paris cedex 04.

Tel: 42 77 12 33.

Open: Monday to Friday noon–10pm, at weekends 10am–10pm.

Closed Tuesday.

Admission charge.

Métro Rambuteau, Châtelet, Hôtel de Ville.

Nearby:

Quartier de l'Horloge

Saint-Merri Church

place Stravinsky

Fontaine des Innocents

Les Halles

Musée de l'Histoire de France

Musée de la Chasse et de la Nature

Tour St-Jacques

Hôtel de Ville.

Churches

Stunning window, St-Germain-de-l'Auxerrois

ST-ETIENNE-DU-MONT

Begun in 1492, the church was only completed in 1626, and its originality lies in its harmonious combination of styles: the chancel and the tower are late Gothic and the Renaissance façade is unique with its three superimposed pediments. Inside, the church is well lit by a row of windows replacing the traditional triforium. The magnificent roodscreen, framed by two graceful open spiral staircases, was built at the beginning of the 16th-century by Antoine Beaucorps according to drawings by Philibert Delorme. Notice also the beautiful pulpit, dating from 1650, and some attractive 16th century stained glass behind it. Further along, past the roodscreen on the right, is St Genevieve's shrine, containing relics of the patron saint of Paris. The philosopher and mathematician, Pascal and the playwright, Racine, are buried behind the chancel.

Place Ste-Geneviève, 75005, next to the Panthéon. Closed: Mondays in July and August. Métro Cardinal-Lemoine.

ST-EUSTACHE

This was the parish church of Les Halles and now that the old food market has gone, it can be seen from afar. In 1532 work started on an imposing Gothic building modelled on Notre-Dame and dedicated to St Eustace. Although it took 100 years to build, the original plans were followed to the letter, and it was a truly Gothic church that was consecrated in 1637. Unfortunately, the 18th-century neoclassical façade that replaced the original one has rather spoilt the overall effect. Many famous people are connected with St-Eustache: Richelieu and Molière were baptised within its walls; the latter was also buried

there, as were the author, La Fontaine, Colbert, Louis XIV's finance minister, and the composer, Rameau. The dimensions of the building are even more impressive from the inside than the outside. Notice the unusual height of the double aisles, the fine vault and the stained-glass windows in the chancel, dating from 1631 and featuring St Eustace among the apostles. The church is decorated with execptional monuments and fine works of art, including *Les Pèlerins d'Emmaüs,* an early Rubens; it also has a strong musical tradition.
Rue du Jour, 75001, next to the Forum des Halles. Métro Les Halles.

ST-GERMAIN DES PRES

This was the church of a powerful Benedictine abbey, a great centre of learning, which owned most of the Left Bank until the 17th century. The abbey buildings were destroyed during the 1789 Revolution, but the Romanesque church was saved and restored in the 19th century. It offers an original mixture of styles: the chancel and nave are Romanesque with Gothic vaulting, the massive tower acquired a steeple in the 19th century, and the original porch is masked by a door added in 1607. Inside, the chancel and ambulatory are the most interesting parts: notice the traditional carvings on the capitals and the ornamental triforium; the marble shafts of its columns come from the original 6th-century church.
Place St-Germain-des-Prés, 75006. Métro St-Germain-des-Prés.

ST-GERMAIN-L'AUXERROIS

The church was built in the 12th century, but has been continually remodelled for 400 years. As a result it

St-Eustache: imposing inside and out

has a Romanesque belfry, a Gothic chancel and a late-Gothic porch, while the aisle round the chancel is Renaissance. It is unfortunately associated with one of the darkest episodes of French history. In 1572, its bells gave the signal for the Massacre of St Bartholomew when thousands of Protestants were murdered as a result of a plot between the Cardinal, Duc de Guise, Catherine de Médicis, Charles IX and the future Henri III. Inside there are some interesting works of art, including a 16th-century Flemish reredos in the fourth chapel on the left of the nave, 15th-century stained-glass in the transept and the rose windows, and a polychrome statue of St-Germain in front of the chancel.
Place du Louvre, 75001. Métro Louvre.

Churches

ST-GERVAIS-ST-PROTAIS

Dedicated to two Roman officers martyred under Nero, this church offers an interesting contrast of styles: the main part is late Gothic with a three-tiered classical façade. Inside there are beautifully carved stalls, 16th- and 17th-century stained glass and a fine 17th-century organ.
Place St-Gervais, 75004. Closed: Mondays. Métro Hôtel de Ville.

St-Julien-le-Pauvre, see page 71.
St-Louis-des-Invalides, see page 69.
St-Louis-en-l'Ile, see page 23.

Bathed in light: St-Gervais St-Protais

ST-MEDARD

This late-Gothic church was completed in the 17th century. Inside there is a 16th-century triptych, as well as other paintings of the French school and an interesting 17th-century organ loft.
Rue Mouffetard, 75005. Closed: Mondays. Métro Censier-Daubenton.

ST-MERRI

This is another late-Gothic church, completed in 1612. The interior was considerably remodelled under Louis XV and the only original features are the stained-glass windows in the chancel. The composer, Camille St-Saëns, used to play on the 17th-century organ, and there are regular concerts in the summer.
Rue de la Verrerie, 75004. Métro Hôtel de Ville or Les Halles.

St-Nicolas-du-Chardonnet,
see page 25.
St-Paul-St-Louis, see page 79.
St-Pierre-de-Montmartre,
see page 81.

ST-ROCH

This is a fine example of classical architecture. Its foundation stone was laid by Louis XIV in 1653, but work was delayed through lack of funds and it was not completed until the 18th century. The façade, in the Jesuit style, dates from 1735. In 1795, Bonaparte charged a group of royalist rebels and the bullet holes can still be seen on the façade.
Rue St-Honoré, 75001. Closed: Sundays except between 5pm–6.30pm. Métro Pyramides or Tuileries.

ST-SEVERIN

Situated in one of the oldest districts of Paris, St-Séverin is named after a hermit who lived in the area in the 6th century. Work on the present building began in the 13th century and went on until 1530. Thus the façade and part of the nave are basically early Gothic, while the rest is late Gothic. In 1681, the Grande Mademoiselle, Louis XIV's cousin, had the chancel altered by the famous architect, Le Brun. Furthermore, the 13th-century west door originally belonged to a nearby church, which was demolished in 1839. Inside, the most remarkable feature is the double ambulatory with its spiral central columns, looking like palm trees under the ribbed vaulting. There is beautiful 16th-century stained glass in the upper windows and modern stained glass by Bazaine in the chapels at the east end.
Rue des Prêtres-St-Séverin, 75005. Open: Monday to Friday. Métro St-Michel or Cluny-Sorbonne.

ST-SULPICE

The church was originally built by the Abbey of St-Germain-des-Prés as a parish church for the surrounding area.

The unusually long church of St-Roch

The present building was started in 1646 and many architects worked on it until 1732, when it was decided to abandon the austere classical style. The Florentine architect, Servandoni, was selected to give the church an Italian-style façade. As you enter, you will notice two giant shells mounted on supports carved by Pigalle; they were offered by the Venetian Republic in 1745. The first chapel on the right as you face the chancel has remarkable murals full of romantic inspiration, painted by Delacroix between 1849 and 1861 (see page 27).
Place St-Sulpice, 75006, near the Luxembourg and St-Germain-des-Prés. Métro St-Sulpice. The Musée Delacroix is near by.

St-Thomas-d'Aquin, see page 35.
Ste-Chapelle, see page 103.

THE BUTTE ST-ROCH

The church of St-Roch was originally built on a hillock upon which stood several windmills. The butte was levelled off as part of Baron Haussmann's ambitious town-planning programme and the windmills all disappeared, except one, the Moulin Radet. This was removed to another high position, the Butte Montmartre, where you can still see it, in rue Lepic!

Ile-de-la-Cité

*I*t is no coincidence that the history of Paris began on this small, boat-shaped island in the middle of the Seine, for a long time the only means of communication. Although the river has lost its once essential role, this tiny strip of land, known as the Ile-de-la-Cité, has remained the heart of the great metropolis that developed around it.

Lutetia

This was the name given to the city by the first known settlers, the Parisii: it was a Celtic word meaning 'a dwelling surrounded by water'.

Ile-de-la-Cité, ancient heart of Paris

The 'Cité'

The Romans brought organisation and prosperity, but after the fall of the Roman Empire, the small island was in peril once again. Although it miraculously escaped the Huns, the Franks besieged it and eventually conquered it. When King Clovis made it his capital in 508, it became known as the 'Cité'. Its renewed prosperity was soon threatened by Norman raids and the city was sacked several times until Eudes, count of Paris, reinforced its fortifications and successfully defended it in 885. For more than 100 years afterwards, however, the town remained within the perimeter of the island.

The role of the cathedral

As a centre of learning, the cathedral played an essential role in maintaining the influence of the Cité after the town began to spread along the banks of the river. Schools flourished between the north side of Notre-Dame and the Seine, an area that belonged to the canons of the cathedral. Abélard was among the many students drawn to the Cité by the reputation of its teaching, and it was in the cloister school that he first met Heloïse. By the end of the 13th century, there were no fewer than 22 chapels and churches in the vicinity of the cathedral.

The supreme court

From the 14th century onwards, the kings of France ceased to live in the Cité, preferring the Louvre and other royal residences outside Paris. The royal palace became the seat of the supreme court of justice. During the Terror, the dreaded *Tribunal révolutionnaire* held its sessions there, next door to the notorious Conciergerie.

Nearby:

Ile St-Louis,

see page 23

Churches of

St-Séverin and

St-Julien-le-Pauvre

Picturesque streets

round place St-Michel

Ste-Chapelle, see

page 103

Musée de Cluny

Notre-Dame

Cathedral,

see page 96.

The Conciergerie, its beauty belies its history

A quiet revolution

The island has changed considerably since the Middle Ages, but its most spectacular remodelling took place during the second half of the 19th century, when the area round the cathedral was cleared of almost all its medieval houses and began to look as it does today.

The Palais de Justice

This part of the old royal palace, many times destroyed by fire and considerably extended in the 19th century, has completely lost its medieval aspect, but it is still worth walking across the main courtyard to the bustling Galerie Marchande to get the feel of the place, before visiting the Ste-Chapelle and the Conciergerie.
Palais de Justice, 4 boulevard du Palais, 75001. Open: 9am–5pm.

The Conciergerie

This is the oldest part of the former royal palace. Bordering the Seine along the quai de l'Horloge, it is most striking seen from the Right Bank. It gets its name from the *concierge* (caretaker) who looked after the royal residence and was allowed to levy taxes. The building already served as a prison before the revolution and, during the Terror, it held such famous prisoners as Marie-Antoinette and Danton. Guided tours take you through the Salle des Gardes and the impressive Salle des Gens d'Armes with superb Gothic vaulting to the vast kitchens, the Galerie des Prisonniers and Marie-Antoinette's cell.
Conciergerie, 1 quai de l'Horloge, 75001. Tel: 43 54 30 06. Open: June to August 9.30am–6.30pm, September, April and May 9.30am–6pm, October 10am–4.30pm. Admission charge.

The Concorde

*T*he place de la Concorde or la Concorde, as it is simply called, is undoubtedly the most splendid square in Paris. Its impressive size, harmonious proportions and superbly elegant setting are the striking features of this true masterpiece of town planning. Because of its strategic position at the crossroads of the main east-west and north-south flows of traffic, it gets very congested at times.

A royal square

The square was commissioned by the aldermen of Paris as a token of their admiration for Louis XV. Ambitious plans submitted by the architect Jacques-Ange Gabriel were approved and a vast area of over 8 hectares of drained marshland was chosen on the edge of town. The square, which was built over a period of 20 years from 1755 to 1775, was originally surrounded by a moat and balustrade, and an equestrian statue of Louis XV by Bouchardon was placed in its centre.

Tragic beginnings

Before work was completed, tragedy struck: in 1770, a huge crowd had gathered on the square to celebrate the wedding of Marie-Antoinette and the future Louis XVI, when panic caused over 100 people to be crushed to death in the moat. Twenty-two years later, the guillotine was set up on the square, which had been renamed place de la Révolution. In 1795, the dreaded instrument was dismantled and the square renamed place de la Concorde as a symbol of hope and peace!

Reconciliation

It was not until 1836 that the name was adopted for good. The square was partly redesigned by the architect Hittorff and the decoration completed. King Louis-Philippe decided against another statue in the centre and chose instead a neutral monument, a 3,000-year-old Egyptian obelisk.

The obelisk

The obelisk, which comes from the temple of Luxor, was a gift from the viceroy of Egypt, Muhammad Ali. It is covered with hieroglyphs which detail the life of Rameses II and the drawings on the base depict the process of dismantling and transporting it, and erecting on its present site. The two large fountains are modelled on those in St Peter's Square in Rome.

The views from the centre of the square are magnificent. To the west are the Champs-Elysées and the Arc de Triomphe, to the east the Tuileries Gardens, the Arc de Triomphe du Carrousel and the Louvre beyond, to the north the rue Royale, closed off by the Madeleine, and to the south, the Pont de la Concorde and the Assemblée Nationale across the river.

The twin mansions

The colonnades of the two identical buildings marking the entrance to the rue Royale were modelled on that of the Louvre. The Hôtel de la Marine is on the right as you face the Madeleine and the Hôtel Crillon on the left. This is now a world famous luxury hotel, but in 1778, soon after it was built, it was the venue for the signing of an important treaty between France and the newly founded United States of America.

Statues round the square

To complete the decoration, eight statues representing various French towns stand in the corners of the square.

Outside the Tuileries gates are two figures on winged horses by Coysevox, representing Fame and Mercury, and, to complement them, the famous *Chevaux de Marly* by Coustou were specially brought from Louis XIV's castle to mark the entrance to the Champs-Elysées. Both sets are now replicas as the marble originals are in the Louvre.

La Concorde, once far from peaceful, offers grand views of the city

Nearby:

The Madeleine

Place Vendôme

Jardin des Tuileries

Musée de l'Orangerie

Musée d'Orsay

Petit Palais and Grand Palais

Assemblée Nationale, 128 rue de l'Université, 75007. Tel: 40 63 63 08. Free guided tours at 10am, 2pm and 3pm. Métro Concorde.

Faubourg St-Germain

*T*his elegant district bordering the Seine between the fashionable St-Germain-des-Prés and the stately Hôtel des Invalides, had its heyday in the 18th century. Two main thoroughfares, boulevard St-Germain and boulevard Raspail, cut across it, carrying fast-moving traffic, while the side streets, taken over by ministries, embassies and official residences, are wrapped in the kind of secluded atmosphere usually found in museums. Indeed, beautifully restored mansions of all sizes (some of them still privately owned) line the streets.

An aristocratic district

The name *faubourg* (suburb) is the only reminder of the area's suburban beginnings, when it was open countryside surrounding the Abbey of St-Germain des Prés. Around 1680, the aristocracy and the wealthy started to move in and, in the space of 50 years, the Faubourg had supplanted the Marais as the most fashionable residential district.

The busy boulevard St-Germain

The Palais Bourbon

The seat of the Assemblée Nationale consists of two 18th-century mansions: the Hôtel de Bourbon built for one of Louis XIV's illegitimate daughters and

GRANDS BOULEVARDS

These wide thoroughfares, slicing through the heart of the capital between the place de l'Opéra and the place de la Bastille, make you feel the real pace of Parisian life. Having replaced obsolete fortifications at the end of the 17th century, the Boulevard became a popular place for strolling. However, a marked difference soon developed between east and west, the latter being the fashionable end!

Today it is still fascinating to notice the change as you walk east from the Opéra. Just off the boulevard des Italiens on the right is the Opéra Comique specialising in light opera. In the boulevard Montmartre on the left is the Musée Grévin, the famous waxworks, while on either side of the boulevard are two 19th-century shopping arcades.

Further east, two 17th-century monumental gates mark the entrance to the boulevard St-Denis and the boulevard St-Martin. South of the boulevard de Bonne Nouvelle is a rather seedy district called le Sentier, a centre of the wholesale trade in fabrics and ready-made clothes.

Places of interest:

Musée d'Orsay,

see page 86

Musée de la Légion

d'Honneur, see

page 34

Musée Rodin, see

page 95

Nearby:

Invalides, see page 68

Church of St-Germain

des Prés, see page 55

Musée Delacroix,

see page 27.

The Hôtel Biron houses the Musée Rodin

the Hôtel de Lassay. The two were joined in 1764 and a Greek-style façade was added in the 19th century to match that of the Madeleine. On the place du Palais Bourbon, the original façade has kept its 18th-century appearance. *128 rue de l'Université, 75007. Tel: 40 63 63 08. Free guided tours start at 10am, 2pm and 3pm. Métro Chambre des Députés or Invalides.*

Streets of special interest
The general plan of the district is very neat, the main *hôtels* (private residences) having been built along five parallel streets. Nearer the river is rue de Lille with the Hôtel de Seignelay at no 80, now the Ministère du Commerce, and the Hôtel de Beauharnais, now the German Ambassador's residence; both

were built in 1714. Next comes rue de l'Université, so called because the land once belonged to the university, with some of the earliest mansions: no 78, built in 1687 and no 51 dating from 1707. The rue St-Dominique lost a few of its 18th-century houses when the boulevard St-Germain was opened. In rue de Grenelle, the most imposing mansion at no 110, dating from 1778, is now occupied by the Ministère de l'Education Nationale; the beautiful Fontaine des Quatre Saisons is at no 57 (see page 65) and next door, the Hôtel Bouchardon is being converted into a museum of modern art. The Hôtel Biron (Musée Rodin) and the Hôtel Matignon (Prime Minister's residence) in rue de Varenne are probably the two most beautiful mansions of the whole district.

Fountains

*P*aris has many public fountains of all shapes and sizes, faithfully reflecting the architectural style of their time. Some, like the Fontaine des Quatre Saisons in the Faubourg St-Germain, were once the only means of water supply in the whole district. Others, like the Fontaine des Quatre Points Cardinaux on place St-Sulpice, were purely ornamental.

FONTAINE DU CHATELET

This is one of the 15 fountains that Napoleon had built in the city. Dating from 1808, it is sometimes referred to as the Fontaine de la Victoire because it commemorates the Emperor's victories in Italy and Egypt. Most often, though, it is called the Fontaine du Palmier because its column suggests a palm tree.
Place du Châtelet, 75001, near the Hôtel de Ville. Métro Châtelet.

The Fontaine des Quatre Points Cardinaux

FONTAINE CUVIER

This very ornate fountain is dedicated to Georges Cuvier, the 19th-century zoologist who founded the study of comparative anatomy. Notice the crocodile turning its head round, something crocodiles apparently cannot do!
Corner of rue Linné and rue Cuvier, 75005, near the Jardin des Plantes. Métro Jussieu or Monge.

FONTAINE DES INNOCENTS

This Renaissance fountain gets its name from the 12th-century Sts-Innocents church demolished at the end of the 18th century. Built in 1550 at the corner of the rue St-Denis by the architect Pierre Lescot and the sculptor Jean Goujon, it was later moved to the centre of the square and restored in 1865, when the original reliefs round the base were removed to the Louvre.
Square des Innocents, 75001, near Les Halles. Métro Les Halles.

FONTAINE LOUVOIS

This ornamental fountain by Visconti is a typical example of the decorative style used in urban architecture during the 19th century. The statues represent four French rivers: the Seine, Loire, Saône and Garonne.
Square Louvois, 75002, near the Bibliothèque Nationale. Métro Bourse.

FONTAINE DE MEDICIS

This is the most romantic fountain in
Paris and one of the main attractions of
the Jardin du Luxembourg. Built in
1624 by Salomon de Brosse for Marie de
Médicis, Henri IV's widow, it is in the
Italian style fashionable at the time.
*Jardin du Luxembourg, 75006. Métro
Odéon, RER Luxembourg.*

FONTAINE MOLIERE

Situated at the intersection of rues de
Richelieu and Molière, this fountain is
dedicated to the famous 17th-century
playwright who died a few yards away at
no 40 rue de Richelieu. Built by Visconti
in 1844, it shows the writer deeply
absorbed in his thoughts (see page 33).
*Rue de Richelieu, 75001, near the Palais-
Royal. Métro Palais-Royal or Pyramides.*

FONTAINE DE L'OBSERVATOIRE

This impressive bronze fountain by
Davioud dates from 1873. It depicts the
different parts of the world – Europe,
Asia, Africa and America – but not
Oceania which would have spoilt the
symmetry of the composition. It is also
called Fontaine des Quatre Parties du
Monde.
*Avenue de l'Observatoire, 75006, south of
the Luxembourg gardens. RER Port-Royal
or Luxembourg.*

FONTAINE DES QUATRE POINTS CARDINAUX

Standing in the centre of the charming
place St-Sulpice, this fountain is the
work of the architect Visconti. Facing
the four cardinal points of the compass
are the busts of four well-known men of
the church who never became cardinals.
*Place St-Sulpice, 75006. Métro St-Sulpice,
Mabillon or Odéon.*

The baroque Médicis fountain

FONTAINE DES QUATRE SAISONS

The street is too narrow to get a good
view of this beautiful 18th-century
fountain carved by Bouchardon. In the
centre, the city of Paris looks down on
the rivers Seine and Marne, while on
either side, are figures representing the
seasons.
*57 rue de Grenelle, 75007, at the heart of
the Faubourg St-Germain. Métro Rue du
Bac.*

FONTAINE ST-MICHEL

This monumental fountain was built by
Davioud during the Second Empire and
is typical of the ornate style in fashion at
the time. It is the favourite meeting-
place of young Parisians.
*Place St-Michel, 75005, in the Latin
Quarter. Métro St-Michel.*

LES HALLES

This is very much an up-and-coming district, developing round the ultra-modern Forum des Halles and rapidly regaining the popularity it lost as a result of the departure of the colourful but obsolete food market that gave the area its name (the word *halles* means covered market). Combined with that of Beaubourg near by, its renovation, undertaken during the 1970s has proved a great success both socially and culturally.

Tradition versus modernisation

There was much controversy about the destruction of the 19th-century Pavillons Baltard housing the old market, for which Parisians suddenly discovered a deep attachment. Firmly-rooted traditions were being threatened, they felt, and would be lost for ever in the pursuit of improbable benefits. However, the planners won and work went ahead.

Forum des Halles

The originality of the complex lies in the fact that there is little to be seen from the street: galleries on four levels run round a huge crater, which provides ample daylight in the central square. From there, a maze of underground 'streets', lined with shops, snack-bars and restaurants, and with direct access to the métro, covers an area of 7 hectares; large maps are available on each level to direct you to the shops of your choice (see page 31). There are two museums on level 1: the Nouveau Musée Grévin, an annexe of the waxworks in the boulevard Montmartre, depicting Paris at the turn of the century; and the Musée Francais de l'Holographie.

In the newest part of the complex, beyond the place Carrée on level 3, a cultural and commercial area includes an auditorium, a video library and the Parc Océanique Cousteau, as well as sports facilities and a glass swimming-pool.

Old streets

At ground level, round the gardens, which offer a pleasant contrast to the feverish underground activity, the old streets have preserved the character of the former market district and many of the food shops, cafés and restaurants are still there.

Forum des Halles, 75001; métro Les Halles. Musée Grévin, level 1. Tel: 40 26 28 50. Open: weekdays 10.30am–6.45pm, Sunday 1pm–7.00pm. Admission charge. Musée de l'Holographie, level 1. Tel: 40 39 96 83. Same opening times. Admission charge.

HOTEL DE VILLE

Although the present building is fairly recent, the site has always played an essential role in the history of the capital. In the Middle Ages, the square in front of the town hall was called the place de Grève because it sloped down to the river (*grève* means shore). Throughout the Ancien Régime, the site was used for public executions. In 1871, the original town hall was destroyed by fire at the same time as the Tuileries palace.

The present building, in neo-Renaissance style, dates from 1882. Its decoration is very elaborate, as was the fashion at the turn of the century: numerous statues adorn the façade, and inside, at the top of a splendid staircase, there are beautiful reception rooms with crystal chandeliers and paintings by Laurens and Puvis de Chavannes.

Rue de Lobau, 75004. Tel: 42 76 40 40. Free guided tours every day 10.30am (ring for confirmation); entrance by the north door. Métro Hôtel de Ville. Hotel de Ville

Left: A popular commercial and cultural complex, Les Halles

Hôtel de Ville

LE VENTRE DE PARIS

The 'belly of Paris' was the evocative name given to the area in the 19th century by the novelist Emile Zola. At that time, it had already been the main food supply centre of the city for centuries, constantly growing until it reached bursting point. The Pavillons Baltard, built between 1854 and 1866, gave the market a new lease of life. However, 100 years later, the market area became congested again and, as there was no more room for expansion, the 'belly' of Paris moved out of town to Rungis.

Invalides

*T*his imposing group of buildings is an outstanding example of 17th century classical architecture, situated at the end of a vast oblong open space stretching across from the Seine. Like Versailles, it epitomises the strength and confidence of the French monarchy under Louis XIV. Moreover, the whole surrounding area, with its wide tree-lined avenues, the Faubourg St-Germain on one side and the Champ de Mars on the other, adds to the impression of space and grandeur. Sought after by wealthy Parisians, it has become a quiet, secluded residential district.

The Dôme church with its gilded cupola

A pensioner's home!

At the beginning of his reign, Louis XIV had difficulty in establishing himself on the throne of France, and realised the importance of a strong army. However, recruitment was difficult, because of the appalling conditions faced by wounded soldiers. In order to encourage potential recruits, the king decided in 1670 to found a hospital and pension home for 4,000 invalid ex-soldiers. Work started in 1671 and lasted for five years.

A shining monument

The king then commissioned the young architect Jules Hardouin-Mansart to design a church with a magnificent gilt dome. In 1840, after years of negotiation with the British Government, Napoleon's remains were returned to France and officially buried in the Eglise du Dôme and Les Invalides became a symbol of the emperor's glory.

The Esplanade des Invalides

The best way to approach the Invalides is from the Pont Alexandre III (see page 51). The vast esplanade designed by Robert de Cotte at the beginning of the 18th century, is 500m long and 250m wide. From here you can enjoy sweeping views of the harmonious ensemble of buildings. A formal garden, surrounded by a dry moat, has 17th- and 18th-century bronze heavy guns; beyond it, the impressive doorway, flanked by twin pavilions, is adorned by an equestrian statue of Louis XIV, dating from 1815.

The Cour d'Honneur

The paved courtyard is lined with arcades on two storeys. Four pavilions

Nearby:

Palais Bourbon

Musée Rodin

Faubourg St-Germain,

see page 62

Champ de Mars

Tour Eiffel,

see page 108

Pont Alexandre III,

see page 51

Invalides still houses old veterans

surmounted by carved pediments have dormer windows adorned with trophies, and in the four corners, at roof level, there are carved horses trampling the emblems of war. More heavy guns complete this imposing setting. On either side of the courtyard are the collections of the Musée de l'Armée (see museums page 88), while, at the end, is the entrance to St-Louis church.

ST-LOUIS-DES-INVALIDES

This is the original church by Libéral Bruant, also known as the soldiers' church, a cold building decorated only with flags and standards taken from the enemy. The Eglise du Dôme is visible through a glass panel behind the altar. The magnificent 17th-century organ was used for the première of Berlioz's *Requiem* in 1837.
Open: 10am–5pm.

EGLISE DU DOME

Begun in 1677, the Eglise du Dôme was completed in 1735. The tiered façade with Doric and Corinthian columns is adorned with statues of St-Louis, Charlemagne and the four virtues, and

further enhanced by the well-proportioned dome. The interior is magnificently decorated with different marbles, painted cupolas, columns and low reliefs. All round the church, in the side chapels, are the tombs of several of Napoleon's generals as well as those of Turenne, Lyautey and Foch .
Hôtel des Invalides, 75007. Métro Invalides, Latour-Maubourg or Varenne. Eglise du Dôme and Musée de l'Armée. Tel: 45 55 37 70. Open: 10am–5pm. Admission charge.

NAPOLEON'S TOMB

In 1861, the architect Visconti imagined an extremely dramatic and most effective setting for the Emperor's tomb. An open crypt was dug and in its centre the red porphyry sarcophagus was placed on a base of green granite from the Vosges. A balustrade running all the way round allows visitors to get a very good view.

Latin Quarter

*T*his is one of the oldest districts of Paris, rich in traditions going back to the Middle Ages, yet teeming with new ideas launched by its lively young population.

Situated on the Left Bank, opposite the Ile-de-la-Cité, the district spreads from the place St-Michel uphill to the Montagne Ste-Geneviève dominated by the Panthéon and the Sorbonne. A free and easy atmosphere pervades the whole area.

The Gallo-Roman city

Roman public buildings were concentrated on the Left Bank, just across the river from the Ile-de-la-Cité occupied by the Celts. Ruins of public baths were discovered next to the Hôtel de Cluny and those of an amphitheatre in the vicinity of the Jardin des Plantes. At the end of the 3rd century hordes of barbarians burned down the whole Left Bank, halting development there for a long time.

Architectural detail at the Sorbonne

A universal language

In the 12th century, several teachers and students broke away from the cathedral schools of the Ile-de-la-Cité and established themselves on the Left Bank. Their action soon led to the foundation of the university of Paris in 1215. Before the end of the 13th century, there were several colleges on the Montagne Ste-Geneviève welcoming students from the French provinces and other parts of Europe. These early Europeans spoke Latin, a practice which lasted until 1789.

THE SORBONNE

This was the first and most successful of the many colleges that flourished in pre-revolutionary Paris. From very humble beginnings in 1253, it developed into a reputed centre of theological studies and became the seat of the powerful university. Its prestige and popularity have survived to this day. The 17th-century buildings were extensively remodelled and enlarged at the end of the 19th century. The Sorbonne church, which is open only on special occasions, dates from the beginning of the 17th century. It contains the white marble tomb of Cardinal Richelieu.

Sorbonne: for free guided tour apply in writing to Madame Lévy, Rectorat de Paris, 45 rue des Ecoles, 75005.

ST-JULIEN-LE-PAUVRE

There has been a church on this site since the 6th century, as it was on the route followed by pilgrims on their way to Santiago de Compostela. The present building, dating from the late 12th century, was the university church from the 13th to the 16th century. St-Julien is now a Greek Orthodox church. Its style is transitional, partly Romanesque and partly Gothic, with a 17th-century façade.
St-Julien-le-Pauvre, rue St-Julien, 75005. Métro St-Michel.

HOTEL DE CLUNY

This is one of the best examples of domestic medieval architecture. It was

Faculty building at the Sorbonne

HELOISE AND ABELARD

A tragic love story has forever united the names of Canon Fulbert's niece Héloïse and a brilliant young teacher from Brittany called Abélard. About 100 years before the foundation of the Sorbonne, Abélard became Héloïse's tutor at her uncle's request. Their love soon blossomed, they eloped, got married and had a son. When they returned to Paris, Canon Fulbert decided to punish Abélard by having him castrated. Abélard became a monk and a famous teacher while Héloïse took the veil, but their love survived and they went on writing passionate letters to each other. They were buried in the same grave inside the monastery that Abelard had founded and of which Héloïse had subsequently become the abbess. Much later their remains were transferred to a single grave in the cimetière du Père Lachaise.

---

built in the 15th century for the abbots of the famous Cluny Abbey on the site of the ruined Roman baths. The style of the house is already inspired by the Renaissance, best observed from the main courtyard. The central building has high windows and an elaborate balustrade with impressive gargoyles, while the main staircase winds up a pentagonal tower. Inside, the Musée de Cluny covers all aspects of medieval art (see page 90).
Hôtel de Cluny, 6 place Paul Painlevé, 75005. Tel: 43 25 62 00. Open: 9.30am–12.30pm, 2pm–5.15pm. Closed: Tuesday. Admission charge. Métro Cluny-La Sorbonne.

Louvre

Situated on the Right Bank, within a stone's throw of the Ile-de-la-Cité, the Louvre expanded according to the whim of successive French monarchs and reached such proportions that it is today one of the world's largest royal palaces. Yet it is not its architectural merit that attracts visitors, but the great museum within its walls. The current Grand Louvre project, however, designed to modernise and smarten it up, has recently caught public attention. Work is still going on, but already the glass pyramid erected in the open courtyard has given rise to controversy, and has renewed interest in the building's 'threatened' architectural beauty.

THE LOUVRE PALACE

The building was consistently extended westwards, away from the congested part of the city.

The medieval fortress

The original castle, built by King Philippe-Auguste at the end of the 12th century, was just a massive keep surrounded by a wall and towers, designed as part of the city's fortifications.

It became a royal residence when Charles V extended the city further west and protected it with new fortifications. Remains of this fortress were discovered under the Cour Carrée, and have been excavated recently as part of the Grand Louvre scheme (access through the museum).

The Renaissance palace

Until the 16th century, the Louvre was neglected in favour of less austere residences in the Marais or on the Loire; then Francis I had part of the obsolete fortress razed and in 1546 he commissioned Pierre Lescot to build a new palace. Lescot worked on it until his death in 1571, entrusting the decoration to the sculptor Jean Goujon.

The Tuileries

It was Catherine de Médicis, Henri II's widow, who initiated the extension of the Louvre westwards. She commissioned Philibert Delorme to build a new palace close to the Louvre. But superstition prevented the queen from settling in the Tuileries Palace – an astrologer told her she would die there! In 1871 it was burned down and had to be demolished.

The Galerie du Bord de l'Eau

Catherine de Médicis had originally intended to link the two palaces by way of a long wing parallel to the river, but these plans were abandoned until Henri IV's accession to the throne. He completed the link in 1608 by having the Galerie du Bord de l'Eau and the Pavillon de Flore built.

The Cour Carrée

Louis XIII and Louis XIV concentrated their efforts on the Cour Carrée. In 1624, the architect Lemercier built the Pavillon de l'Horloge in the centre of the west wing, which he extended by another building faithfully matching that of Pierre Lescot. The other three sides were completed by Louis XIV's

Palais du Louvre, 75001. For opening times, see Musée du Louvre page 74. Métro Palais-Royal.

Nearby:

Tuileries Gardens

Louvre des Antiquaires

Oratoire du Louvre

Churches of St-Roch and St-Germain-L'Auxerrois

Pont des Arts

Musée d'Orsay

Countless masterpieces are on view in the vast halls of the Louvre

architects: Le Vau, Le Brun and Perrault, who also rebuilt the Apollo wing linking the Cour Carrée to the Galerie du Bord de l'Eau. The impressive Colonnade marks the formal entrance to the palace.

Squatters in the Louvre!

Abandoned in favour of Versailles at the end of the 17th century, the palace was neglected and taken over by artists and their families; eventually, an assortment of buildings concealed the beautiful façades which were threatened with dilapidation. However, in 1793, the Galerie du Bord de l'Eau was turned into a museum.

The Carrousel

Napoleon settled in the Tuileries and restored order to the architectural jumble; he also commissioned Percier and Fontaine to build the Arc de Triomphe du Carrousel and a north wing along the rue de Rivoli, which was completed by Napoleon III.

The Grand Louvre

The purpose of this project, which began in 1981, was to create more room for the museum by refurbishing the north wing, formerly occupied by the Ministère des Finances, and to provide badly needed public facilities.

The architect, Pei, consequently designed a vast new underground entrance hall over which stands a glass pyramid. The project is due to be completed in 1995.

The Louvre Museum

*F*rancis I started the royal collection in the 16th century by acquiring 12 paintings by Italian masters including Leonardo Da Vinci's *Mona Lisa,* which is still the most famous of the museum's art treasures. During the reign of Louis XIV, the king's minister, Colbert practised a policy of systematic buying and the collection swelled to more than 2,000 paintings. Meanwhile, the Académie Royale de Peinture et de Sculpture, founded in 1648, was already holding its annual exhibition in the Louvre and artists were granted lodgings in the palace. Shortly after the creation of the museum in 1793, works of art were brought back from Versailles and later Napoleon and his successors continued to enrich the collections with Greek, Assyrian and Egyptian antiquities.

The museum today

The entrance hall, reached by means of an impressive open spiral staircase, or a lift, is well planned. The information desk has leaflets in English, and ground plans. If you are looking for a particular work, ask a member of staff to direct you, since the reorganisation of the museum has not been completed yet and changes occur regularly. There are 18km of corridors so rather than 'do' the Louvre, be selective and decide what you want to see.

The main departments

The museum is divided into three *régions*: Sully, comprising the buildings round the Cour Carrée, Denon, the south wing and Richelieu, the north wing (not open yet). These regions are subdivided into numbered *arrondissements*, identifiable by a colour code. Until the opening of the Richelieu wing, there are only two ways of reaching the different departments. The Sully escalator to the east leads to Oriental antiquities, Egyptian antiquities, *objets d'art* and French paintings from the 14th to the 17th centuries. The Denon escalator to the south leads to Greek, Etruscan and Roman antiquities, the rest of the painting collections, sculpture, prints, drawings, pastels and watercolours.

The medieval moat

The Sully escalator leads directly to rooms depicting the history of the palace and surrounding area; from there you can go to the Sully region, or walk round the moat of the medieval fortress buried under the Cour Carrée. Objects found during the excavations include Charles VI's gilt helmet (14th-century).

Oriental antiquities

This department houses archaeological finds from the valleys of the Euphrates and the Tigris, concerning mainly the Sumerian and Babylonian civilisations, the Elamite and Persian civilisations, the Phoenicians and the Assyrians.

Egyptian antiquities

The great Sphinx in pink granite makes a most impressive introduction to Egyptian art, while the Seated Scribe, dating from around 2500BC, and the bust of Amenophis IV from Karnak are strikingly realistic masterpieces.

Da Vinci's ever intriguing Mona Lisa

Musée du Louvre, Palais du Louvre, 75001, Paris Cedex 01. Tel: 40 20 51 51. Open: 9am–6pm, closed Tuesday and some public holidays. Admission charge. Facilities available: bookshop, auditorium, restaurant and cafeteria which remain open after closing time. Main entrance under the glass pyramid in the Cour Napoléon. Métro Palais-Royal.

Greek, Etruscan and Roman antiquities

You cannot visit the Louvre Museum without seeing the *Venus de Milo*, dating from the 2nd century BC and generally acknowledged as a perfect example of feminine beauty.

Paintings

Several paintings by Leonardo da Vinci, Titian and Raphaël are among the most outstanding works of the Italian school. Flemish and Dutch painters include Rembrandt and Van Dyck. There is also a superbly dramatic *Christ en croix* by El Greco. The French school is strongly represented by de la Tour, Poussin, Watteau, Delacroix and Géricault.

Sculpture

Of special interest are *Les Nymphes* by Jean Goujon, *Les Chevaux de Marly* by Guillaume Coustou, a copy of which guards the entrance to the Champs Elysées, several busts by Houdon, and the *Esclaves* by Michelangelo.

Objets d'art

The Crown Jewels including the Regent, a 140-carat diamond, are usually the biggest attraction here. Among a wealth of other fine pieces are the fine Maximilian tapestries and excellent furniture by Boulle.

Colonial connections, refugees and other immigrant groups are evident in the vibrant, cosmopolitan atmosphere of Paris' ethnic commercial ventures

Today, foreigners account for one-sixth of the capital's population; thus, over the last few decades, the character of certain areas has drastically changed. Some minorities, like the White Russians, are fully assimilated, even if they still get together on occasions. Others, however, live in enclaves that, over the years, have acquired a strong cultural identity.

The Jewish district is situated at the heart of the Marais, within a small quadrangle formed by rue de Rivoli, rue des Francs-Bourgeois, rue Vieille-du-Temple and rue de Sévigné. There has been a Jewish community in this area since the Middle Ages but the arrival in 1962 of a great

large number of Asian immigrants, the majority of them Chinese, settled in the area surrounding the porte de Choisy. The avenue d'Ivry is particularly lively with its cinemas, restaurants, supermarkets and shops that look like pagodas.

Successive waves of immigrants, mainly from Africa, have settled in the Goutte-d'Or district, just east of Montmartre, and now more than 30 nationalities cohabit in deteriorating conditions. Redevelopment is in the air, understandably opposed by the locals, for what will become of the colourful little shops that make a roaring trade selling exotic groceries, junk jewellery and African fabrics etc?

Ethnic Paris

number of Algerian Jews suddenly altered the east European flavour of the district. The rue des Rosiers is very picturesque, with its delicatessens, restaurants, felafel snack bars, and old food shops turned into fashion boutiques.

During the 1960s, tower block flats mushroomed in the 13th *arrondissement* and, as a result, a

The Marais

*T*his is one of the most authentic districts of Paris, with a wealth of 17th-century domestic architecture. It is also a lively area, where traditions are being rediscovered and where variety and contrasts make strolling along its picturesque streets a real pleasure.

Rest your feet, enjoy a drink and watch the world go by at a Marais café

Against all odds!

Only 30 years ago the Marais seemed to have irretrievably sunk back into its murky beginnings! The name suggests marshy land and this is exactly what it was until, in the 13th century, various religious communities, including the Knights Templar, turned it into arable land. At the beginning of the 17th century, Henri IV had the place Royale (now the place des Vosges) built right at the heart of the district and the aristocracy promptly commissioned the most renowned architects to design the splendid mansions (hôtels) seen there today. This was the Marais's golden age! But then fashion changed and the district, deserted by the wealthy in favour of the Faubourg St-Germain, was taken over by shopkeepers and craftsmen, while the beautiful mansions gradually became dilapidated.

A new lease of life

In the early 1960s, the Ministre de la Culture, André Malraux, made the district a protected area and restoration work began straight away. It was a remarkably successful rescue operation.

The Marais assumed its cultural heritage while offering its inhabitants a new quality of life. Some *hôtels* were cleverly converted into flats or turned into museums, new shopkeepers moved in and set up smart boutiques. An artistic revival followed, which is still very apparent. A festival of drama and music takes place annually, while art galleries thrive and multiply.

Interesting streets

It is certainly worth taking your time, and even losing your way, in the side streets north of the rue des Francs-Bourgeois. There are also lively streets, which you don't want to miss. Stretching from one end of the Marais to the other, the rue des Francs-Bourgeois is a commercial street lined with many fine houses, boutiques, cafés and restaurants. The rue des Archives is well known for its fancy leather goods and jewellery. The rue Vieille-du-Temple again has an assortment of restaurants, cafés and quaint shops, and the rue des Rosiers is the picturesque main street of the Jewish Quarter. South of the wide rue St-Antoine, the area of rue St-Paul and the Village St-Paul is a must for antiques lovers.

Some beautiful mansions

The Hôtel Carnavalet in the rue de Sévigné is a Renaissance mansion remodelled by Mansart in the 17th century. Madame de Sévigné lived in it for 20 years and wrote many of her famous letters there. It now houses the Musée Historique de la Ville de Paris.

Across rue des Francs-Bourgeois is the Hôtel de Lamoignon, dating from 1584 and one of the oldest mansions in the district.

At the corner of rue des Archives and rue des Francs-Bourgeois, the Hôtel de Soubise is an early-18th-century residence, but its corbelled turrets are a reminder of the original 14th-century manor-house. Since 1808 it has been the home of the National Archives.

The Hôtel de Sens, in rue du Figuier, is one of the few remaining medieval residences – it was built in the late 15th century. Notice the turrets and the beautiful courtyards.

In rue des Archives, the Hôtel Guénégaud, built in 1650, houses the Musée de la Chasse et de la Nature, which has an interesting collection of arms as well as pictures by Vernet, Oudry and Chardin, and tapestries on the theme of hunting.

St-Paul-St-Louis

This baroque church, completed in 1641, was modelled on the Gesù church in Rome. The interior is well-lit and richly decorated; in the transept there is a *Christ au Jardin des Oliviers* by Delacroix.

Nearby:	Bourgeois, see
Church of St-Paul-	page 91
St-Louis	Musée de la Chasse
Hôtel de Sully,	et de la Nature,
62 rue St-Antoine	60 rue des Archives.
Place des Vosges,	Tel: 42 72 86 43.
see page 100	Open: 10am to
Museums:	12.30pm, 1.30pm–
Carnavalet, Cognacq-	5 30pm.
Jay and Picasso	Closed: Tuesdays.
Hôtel de Soubise, 60	Admission charge.
rue des Francs-	Métro St-Paul

Montmartre

*T*he distinctive white outline of the Sacré-Coeur basilica, visible from almost anywhere in the city, is the universally recognised symbol of Montmartre.

Montmartre is a name that draws on people's imaginations to keep alive the memory of its heyday. For, unlike other districts, la Butte relies entirely on its past image for survival. Quite often it looks like a vast open-air theatre where the décor never changes and the same play is enacted every day!

The case of Montmartre is, of course, unique, for it was its picturesque rural atmosphere and its free and 'easy' life that caught the world's attention at a time when most cities were overwhelmed with industrial squalor. It had nothing to offer except its refreshing simplicity, and its artists. The artists left long ago and there only remained a few cafés and cabarets full of memories, a heritage very difficult to preserve in a rapidly changing city with a growing tourist trade.

The most interesting parts of Montmartre are today centred round rue Lepic and its market, as well as the place des Abbesses and the surrounding area. However, it is well worth strolling along rue des Saules or the place du Tertre early in the morning or off season.

Montmartre, still a village at heart

Bohemian life

It all began in the early 19th century, when a few artists and writers wishing to lead a freer life settled on the Butte: Berlioz, Nerval and Heine were three of the earliest residents. After the Franco-Prussian war of 1870, Montmartre became the centre of Paris's bohemian life, inhabited by impoverished painters and poets and visited by Parisians who flocked into the cabarets, cafés and dance halls. At the turn of the century, the most famous of these establishments were the Chat Noir and the Moulin Rouge at the foot of the hill, the Moulin

TOULOUSE-LAUTREC

Born into the aristocracy and crippled at an early age, Toulouse-Lautrec led a very sad life that only his passion for painting could help him endure. He found the best expression for his talent in scenes of Montmartre's nightlife, sketching its stars with unique realism.

de la Galette half-way up in rue Lepic, La Bonne Franquette at the corner of rue des Saules and rue St-Rustique and the Lapin Agile down on the other side of the hill. Artists like Renoir, Van Gogh and Toulouse-Lautrec, found their inspiration among the enthusiastic spectators and the colourful performers. They were succeeded by Utrillo, Picasso, Braque, Modigliani and many others. This lasted until World War I, when the artists left for Montparnasse

Musée de Montmartre

Number 12 rue Cortot is one of the oldest houses on the Butte, dating from the 17th century. The museum depicts the history of Montmartre through mementoes of its most famous inhabitants. There is a reconstruction of the Café de l'Abreuvoir where Utrillo used to go, and of the study of the composer Charpentier.

St-Pierre-de-Montmartre

This is one of the oldest churches in Paris, once part of the powerful Abbey of Montmartre. Built in the 12th century, it has an 18th-century façade. Inside there are some fine carvings on the Romanesque capitals contrasting with the modern stained glass, as well as four marble columns, probably belonging to a Roman temple that stood on the site.

Cimetière de Montmartre

Access to the cemetery is by a flight of stairs on the left of rue de Caulaincourt, at the end of the bridge as you walk towards the boulevard de Clichy. Ask for a map at the entrance. Many famous artists and writers are buried here, among them the novelists Stendhal and Zola, the composer Berlioz, the poets Heine and Vigny, the painter Degas,

Painter captures the spirit of Montmartre

and, more recently, the film director François Truffaut.

Métro Abbesses or	Closed: Monday.
Lamarck-	Admission charge.
Caulaincourt.	Historical waxworks,
Nearby:	rue Poulbot.
Sacré-Coeur,	Tel: 46 06 78 92.
see page 102	Open: 11am–6.30pm.
Musée de	Admission charge.
Montmartre,	Cimetière de
12 rue Cortot.	Montmartre, rue
Tel: 46 06 61 11.	Caulaincourt. Métro
Open: 2.30pm–6pm.	place de Clichy.

Capital
of the Arts

*Paris remains, reassuringly, a city of
street artists who can provide unique
mementoes of your visit – and perhaps
you'll spot a budding Braque or
Toulouse-Lautrec*

Ever since the 12th century, when students and tutors rejected the stifling teaching of the church and moved to the Left Bank, Paris has been a centre of attraction for artists from all over the world, and the melting-pot of new art movements. This long-standing tradition reached its climax during the second half of the 19th century.

It was after 1870 that Paris really became the world's artistic centre, being both a sanctuary for misunderstood artists, such as Oscar Wilde, and the birthplace of major art movements, such as impressionism.

The 'Bateau-Lavoir' was the romantic name of a shabby wooden building in Montmartre lived in at the turn of the century by poor artists

including Modigliani, Van Dongen, Juan Gris, and above all Picasso and Braque, who developed the cubist style as a reaction against impressionism. Picasso's *Les Demoiselles d'Avignon* was painted here. The artistic life is depicted in Puccini's opera *La Bohème*.

It was at that time too that Diaghilev created his *Ballets russes* and that the première of Stravinsky's *Sacre du Printemps* caused a scandal at the Theâtre des Champs Elysées.

The indecisive period between 1918 and 1939 was marked by the 'lost generation', a group of American writers including Gertrude Stein, Ezra Pound and Ernest Hemingway, while the Exposition Internationale des Arts Décoratifs et Industriels in 1925 launched a new style, Art Déco.

After the difficult post-World-War-II period, Paris is now reclaiming its position as leader in contemporary art. This revival was sparked off by the inauguration of the Centre Pompidou, followed by other major projects such as the Opéra Bastille and La Villette, which offer a new range of artistic experiences.

Montparnasse

*U*nlike Montmartre, this 'other' artists' stronghold was brutally drawn into the 20th century when a major town-planning project remodelled its centre during the 1960s and 1970s.

Olympian heights!

The area was jokingly given the pompous name of Mont Parnasse (Mount Parnassus) in the 17th century by students from the Latin Quarter. In the 18th century it was a place of popular entertainment as bars, restaurants and cabarets, just outside the city boundaries, could serve tax-free wine. The tradition survived even after the district became part of Paris during the second half of the 19th century.

La 'Ruche'

Just before World War I, artists and poets suddenly moved from Montmartre to this unknown Left Bank district which soon came into the limelight, attracting painters and also composers such as Stravinsky and Satie, and, later, the 'lost generation' of American writers. The wine pavilion from the 1900 Exposition Universelle was transferred to the passage de Dantzig by a patron of the arts for the benefit of needy artists; it was given the romantic name of la Ruche (the beehive) and soon welcomed Modigliani, Zadkine, Chagall and Léger. Matisse, Picasso, Braque, Klee, Miro, Ernst, Cocteau and Apollinaire all lived in Montparnasse at one time, their social life revolving round four cafés in the boulevard Montparnasse: La Coupole, Le Select, La Rotonde and Le Dôme. Here they met with Russian political refugees like Lenin and Trotsky.

The old district

This is still centred round the Carrefour Vavin, now the place Pablo-Picasso, where the well-known cafés-restaurants have survived and keep the legend alive, crowded with today's intellectuals and artists. But, whereas the décor has been carefully preserved, the establishments are certainly more up-market now than in the days of Chagall.

Just west of the Cimetière Montparnasse, rue de la Gaîté is, as its name implies, the centre of the district's nightlife. It is lined with cabarets, dance halls and theatres such as the Théâtre de la Gaîté-Montparnasse and the Théâtre Montparnasse.

Cimetière Montparnasse

The main entrance is in the boulevard Edgar-Quinet. Many writers, artists and composers are buried here: among them the poet Baudelaire, the novelist Maupassant, the critic Sainte-Beuve, the philosopher Sartre and his lifelong companion Simone de Beauvoir, the composers César Franck and Saint-Saëns, and the sculptors Rude, Bourdelle and Zadkine. On the eastern edge of the cemetery *The Kiss* is an interesting sculpture by the Romanian artist, Constantin Brancusi who lived in Paris for many years.

Tour Montparnasse

At the heart of the new development stands the 210m high, 59-storey Tour de Maine-Montparnasse. When it was built in the early 1970s, it was Europe's tallest office block and raised fierce controversy at the time. The fastest of the 25 lifts climbs 6m per second, reaching the top

Left: Rue de la Gaîté: old theatres survive despite the street's changing character

floor in 39 seconds. For most Parisians, the tower's only redeeming feature is the splendid panorama from the 56th floor. Across the pink-granite square in front of the tower is the new Gare Montparnasse.

Tour Montparnasse, 33 avenue du Maine, 75015. Tel: 45 38 52 56. Open: 10am –10pm in winter; 9.30am–11pm in summer. Admission charge.

Musée Bourdelle

The museum occupies the house and studio of Antoine Bourdelle, a disciple of Rodin, whose bust is among the exhibits. There are also some very interesting portraits of Beethoven.

Musée Bourdelle, 16 rue Antoine-Bourdelle. Tel: 45 48 67 27. Open: 10am–5.40pm. Closed: Monday. Admission charge.

Musée de la Poste

The museum depicts the history of postal services, and has some fascinating exhibits such as the balloon used during the siege of Paris in 1870. There is also a collection of French stamps and a display of contemporary machines and methods.

Musée de la Poste, 34 boulevard de Vaugirard. Tel: 43 20 15 30. Open: 10am–5pm. Closed: Sunday. Admission charge.

Musée Zadkine

The works of the Russian-born sculptor, Zadkine, are exhibited in the house where he lived for 40 years until his death in 1967. The majority of his works reveal his anxious nature. The various studies he made of Van Gogh are of particular interest.

Musée Zadkine, 100 bis rue d'Assas. Tel: 43 26 91 90. Open: 10am–5 30pm. Closed: Monday. Admission charge.

Musee d'Orsay

*I*deally situated on the Left Bank, opposite the Tuileries Gardens, the recently inaugurated Musée d'Orsay has already taken its rightful place among the top European art museums. It is an unusual museum, housed in a converted railway station, and this allowed the curators to depart from traditional display and to avoid monotony.

Gare d'Orsay

Inaugurated in 1900, the station was built on the site of the Palais d'Orsay which was burnt to the ground during the Commune of 1871. The architect, Victor Laloux, was entrusted with the delicate task of designing a station that would not deface the surrounding area, in particular the Louvre and Tuileries Gardens just across the Seine. He concealed the glass-roofed iron structure behind a beautiful stone façade and adorned it inside with an elaborately decorated coffered ceiling. However, less than 40 years later it had become obsolete, its platforms being too short for new electric trains.

A museum of 19th century art

In 1977 it was finally decided to convert the station into an art museum that would regroup various collections covering the period from 1848 to 1914, including the famous Impressionist collection from the Jeu de Paume. Thus the new museum would make the link between the Louvre and the Musée National d'Art Moderne of the Pompidou Centre. It is an absolute must for anyone interested in 19th-century art.

The museum

When the museum opened in 1986, after a number of setbacks, it was universally acclaimed for the originality of its excellent interior design.

The collections are exhibited in chronological order, on three main levels: the ground floor, the upper floor and the middle floor (in that order). In addition to the permanent collections, there are temporary exhibitions. Ground plans and leaflets in English are available near the entrance.

The **ground floor** is devoted to the period from 1848 to 1880. The sculpture section, in the central gallery, illustrates an interesting progression from the classical style of Pradier *(Sapho)* to the Romantic approach of Carpeaux, who carved the beautiful figures of the Fontaine de l'Observatoire (see page 65). The rooms on the right and left of the gallery form the painting section; on the right, the classical trend is represented by Ingres *(La Source)* and the Romantic trend by Delacroix *(Chasse aux Lions)*. Further on there are some fine Puvis de Chavannes and early Degas. The rooms on the left show the progression from realism with Daumier, Millet *(Les Glaneuses)*, Courbet *(L'Atelier)* and the Barbizon school headed by Corot, towards Impressionism, represented by works painted before 1870: among them the famous *Déjeuner sur l'Herbe* by Manet, *La Pie* and *Femmes au jardin* by Monet. In the architecture section, there is an interesting model of the Opéra Garnier and its district.

1 rue de Bellechasse, 75007. Tel: 40 49 48 14. Open: 10am–6pm; Thursday 10am–9.45pm. Closed: Monday. Admission charge (less crowded early morning). Facilities include: ground floor – bookshop, post office, bureau de change and cloakrooms; upper level – coffee shop; intermediate level – restaurant. Métro Solférino.

The **upper floor** is entirely devoted to Impressionism from 1872 and Post-Impressionism in a splendid festival of light and colour with: *La Gare St-Lazare* and *La Cathédrale de Rouen* by Monet, *Le Moulin de la Galette* and *La Balançoire* by Renoir, *L'Inondation à Port-Marly* by Sisley, *Danseuses Bleues* and *Courses à Longchamp* by Degas. Van Gogh too, influenced by the movement, has his rightful place here, with his sunlit *Chambre de Vincent à Arles;* so does Cézanne, who stands apart as a pioneer of 20th-century painting, for his *Femme à la cafetière* or *Joueurs de cartes* are 'carved' with colour.

Post-Impressionism is represented by Seurat, Toulouse-Lautrec, Henri

See Impressionists and Post-Impressionists before fatigue sets in

Rousseau and his own naïve style, Gauguin *(Le Cheval blanc)* and the school of Pont-Aven, Bonnard, Vuillard and so on.

The **middle floor** painting section is devoted to naturalism and symbolism, which became officially recognised themes at a time when Impressionism was rejected, and to the early 20th century with artists such as Matisse and Bonnard.

The sculpture gallery presents works by Rodin and his successors. The Art Nouveau section is well headed by Gallé, Lalique and Guimard.

Museums

Military history at the Musée de l'Armée

Cité des Sciences et de l'Industrie, see page 114
Maison de Balzac, see page 113
Musée Victor Hugo, see page 101

MUSÉE DE L'ARMÉE

This is one of the most comprehensive military museums in the world. The collections are housed in buildings situated on either side of the main courtyard of Les Invalides (see page 68).

Galerie de l'Occident (west side)

Among the most remarkable exhibits in the ground-floor rooms is Henri II's suit of armour with three interwoven letters, H for Henri, C for Catherine du Médicis

(the queen) and D for Diane de Poitiers (the king's mistress). The first floor is entirely devoted to World War I and World War II, with a video film about D-Day.

Galerie de l'Orient (east side)

On the ground floor there are frescos depicting Louis XIV's campaign in Flanders in 1672 and the famous paintings by Ingres of Napoleon on the day of his coronation, as well as numerous flags and a history of cavalry. On the first floor there are mementoes of Napoleon. The second floor is devoted to the Second Empire and the Franco-Prussian war of 1870.
Hôtel des Invalides, 75007 Paris. Tel: 45 55 37 70. Open: 10am–5pm. Admission charge. Métro Invalides.

MUSÉE D'ART MODERNE DE LA VILLE DE PARIS

The museum is housed in the Palais de Tokyo, built for the 1937 Exposition Universelle. *La Fée Electricité*, painted by Dufy for the occasion, is exhibited in the museum, alongside other works of 20th-century art illustrating the main trends.
Palais de Tokyo, 11 avenue du Président-Wilson, 75016. Tel: 47 23 61 27. Open: 10am–5.30pm. Closed: Monday. Admission charge. Métro Alma-Marceau.

Musée des Arts d'Afrique et d'Oceanie, see page 121

MUSÉE DES ARTS ASIATIQUES-GUIMET

Founded in the 19th century by Emile Guimet, the museum now houses a major collection of Far Eastern art on

three floors. On the ground floor there are some impressive sculptures from Cambodia, including several heads of Buddha. On the first floor there is a wide range of Indian art, exhibits from Pakistan, superb carved ivories from Afghanistan and bronze, jade and lacquered objects from China. On the second floor there are some beautiful Chinese ceramics.
6 place d'Iéna, 75016. Tel: 47 23 61 65. Open: 9.45am–5.15pm. Closed: Tuesday. Admission charge. Métro Iéna.

MUSÉE DES ARTS DÉCORATIFS
The museum is housed in the north wing of the Louvre and has been refurbished recently. The collections are chronologically presented, the 20th-century section being of particular interest with a splendid reconstruction of Jeanne Lanvin's flat, some Dubuffet

Musée d'Art Moderne has changing exhibitions

paintings and sculptures, and glass objects by Gallé and Lalique. There is also a large toy collection.
109 rue de Rivoli, 75001. Tel: 42 60 32 14. Open: Wednesday to Sunday 12.30pm–6pm. Admission charge. Métro Palais-Royal or Tuileries.

MUSÉE DES ARTS DE LA MODE
Housed in the Pavillon de Marsan, this museum, inaugurated in 1985, depicts the history of fashion and costume from the Middle Ages to the present day, with an emphasis on temporary exhibitions.
107 rue de Rivoli, 75001. Tel: 42 60 32 14. Open: Wednesday to Sunday 12.30pm–6pm. Admission charge. Métro Palais-Royal or Tuileries.

Musée des Arts et Traditions Populaires, see page 111
Musée Bourdelle, see page 85
Musée Cernuschi, see page 111
Musée de la Chasse et de la Nature, see page 79
Musée du Cinéma, see page 98

MODERN ART TRENDS
Fauvism: A turn-of-the-century trend characterised by a simplification of form and use of bright colours.
Cubism: An early 20th-century movement concerned with rendering form and volume through geometric shapes.
Abstract art: A movement started in 1910 by Kandinsky rejecting figurative representation of reality. Developed mainly from 1950 onwards, especially in the US with Abstract Expressionism.
Surrealism: A 1920s trend that rejected all conventions and aimed at expressing the subconscious mind.
Realism and New Realism: From 1960 onwards, they mark a return to figurative painting with the introduction of objects from everyday life.

Wood carving of Christ carrying the Cross

MUSÉE DE CLUNY

Housed in one of the few domestic
medieval buildings left in Paris, on the
site of ancient Roman baths (see page
71), this is an exceptionally fine museum
entirely devoted to the Middle Ages.

On the ground floor there are 15th-
and 16th-century tapestries made in
Holland in the *mille fleurs* style.
Particularly worthy of note is a set called
La Vie Seigneuriale, depicting the life of
the aristocracy in the 16th century.

In room VIII, there are some
fragments of sculpture, including 21
heads from the Galerie des Rois that
were originally on the west front of
Notre Dame. Next door is the well-
preserved frigidarium with a fine
example of Roman vaulting.

On the first floor is the museum's
major exhibit: a set of six tapestries from
the late 15th century, called *La Dame à
la Licorne* (the Lady and the Unicorn).

The lovely Gothic chapel contains
another set of tapestries illustrating the
life of St Stephen.
*6 place Paul-Painlevé, 75005. Tel: 43 25
62 00. Open: 9.45am–12.30pm,
2pm–5.15pm. Closed: Tuesday. Admission
charge. Métro Cluny-La Sorbonne, St-
Michel or Odéon.*

MUSÉE COGNAC-JAY

This collection of 18th-century art has
found a proper setting in the recently
renovated Hôtel Donon in the Marais.
Paintings and pastels by Boucher, Frago-
nard, La Tour, Greuze, Tiepolo and
Reynolds and drawings by Watteau are
enhanced by beautiful pieces of furniture
and other objects of the same period.
*8 rue Elzévir, 75003. Tel: 40 27 07 21.
Open: 10am–5.40pm. Closed: Monday.
Admission charge. Métro St-Paul.*

Musée Delacroix, see page 27

MUSÉE GRÉVIN

This waxworks founded in 1882 provides good entertainment for the whole family. There are vivid historical scenes and numerous life-size wax figures of famous people, as well as distorting mirrors.

10 boulevard Montmartre, 75009. Tel: 47 70 85 05. Open: 1pm–7pm. Admission charge. Métro rue Montmartre.

Musée Gustave Moreau, see page 113

MUSÉE HISTORIQUE DE LA VILLE DE PARIS

Housed in the imposing Hôtel Carnavalet, the museum was recently extended to the Hôtel Le-Peletier-de-St-Fargeau and covers the history of Paris from its origins to the present day.

Hôtel Carnavalet

The museum is reached through the monumental doorway and across the courtyard with an equestrian statue of Louis XIV by Coysevox. There are some interesting scenes from Paris life in the 16th century, supported by a host of authentic details such as shop and inn signs. Upstairs are reconstructed rooms from the reigns of Louis XIV, XV and XVI and Madame de Sévigné's apartments.

Hôtel Le-Peletier-de-St-Fargeau

This is linked to the Hôtel Carnavalet and covers the period from the French Revolution; start on the second floor. There are models of the Bastille and the guillotine and objects from everyday life, and a reconstruction of the Temple prison where Louis XVI was held. The ground floor deals with the first half of the 19th century through portraits of people in the limelight. The first floor

follows on with the Second Empire and the great architectural schemes that were carried out during that period. The lifestyle of the early 20th century is presented through reconstructions of rooms such as Marcel Proust's bedroom.

23 rue de Sévigne, 75003. Tel: 42 72 21 13. Open: 10am–5.40pm. Closed: Monday. Admission charge. Métro St-Paul.

Façade of old café, Musée Carnavalet

MUSÉE DE L'HISTOIRE DE FRANCE

This museum, housed in the beautiful Hôtel de Soubise, depicts French history through documents selected from the national archives. Of particular interest are the *Edit de Nantes* of 1598 recognising religious freedom, and its *Révocation* in 1685, which led to the exile of the Huguenots; the *Déclaration des Droits de l'Homme* of 1789 (Declaration of Human Rights); Louis XVI's diary; Napoleon's will and many others. The apartments of the Princess de Soubise have the most exquisite rococo decorations, with paintings by Natoire, Boucher and Van Loo.

60 rue des Francs-Bourgeois, 75003. Tel: 40 27 60 00. Open: 1.45pm–5.45pm. Closed: Tuesday. Admission charge. Métro Rambuteau.

MUSÉE DE L'HOMME

This museum of mankind, housed in the vast Palais de Chaillot, depicts the evolution of the human race since the origin of the species, and presents a comparative study of the different races in their traditional environment.
Place du Trocadéro, 75016. Tel: 45 53 70 60. Open: 9.45am–5.15pm. Closed: Tuesday. Admission charge. Métro Trocadéro.

Tattooed New Zealander, exhibit at the Musée de l'Homme

INSTITUT DU MONDE ARABE

The building situated along the river, facing the Ile St-Louis, is the result of close co-operation between France and 19 Arab countries with the aim of promoting cultural exchanges. The institute houses a reference centre, a video centre, a comprehensive library and a museum (on the 7th floor), which illustrates Arab civilisation from the 9th century onwards. From the cafeteria on the 9th floor there are lovely views of the river.
Rue des Fossés St-Bernard, 75005. Tel: 40 51 38 38. Open: 1pm–8pm. Closed: Monday. Admission charge. Métro Jussieu or Cardinal-Lemoine.

MUSÉE JACQUEMART-ANDRÉ

Although situated right in the centre of town, the museum is in a business area, a little off the visitor's beaten track, but it is well worth making a detour to see its fine collections of Italian Renaissance and 18th-century art, displayed in elegant surroundings. They include paintings by Botticelli, Tintoretto, Ucello's *St George Slaying the Dragon,* sculptures by Donatello, frescos by Tiepolo (over the staircase), 16th-century enamels and ceramics, some beautiful furniture, Beauvais tapestries and paintings by Boucher and Watteau. The museum is closed for major refurbishment and is due to open in January 1993.
158 boulevard Haussmann, 75008. Tel: 45 62 39 94. Open: 1.30pm–5.30pm. Closed: Monday and Tuesday. Admission charge. Métro St-Philippe-du-Roule or Miromesnil.

Musée du Louvre, see page 74
Musée des Lunettes et des Lorgnettes, see page 112

MUSÉE DE LA MARINE

Founded in 1827 by Charles X, the museum now occupies the west wing of

the Palais de Chaillot. With the help of
scale models and actual crafts, it
illustrates all kinds of maritime transport
from battleships to pleasure-boats. There
is an interesting royal toy called the *Louis
XV*, Marie-Antoinette's pleasure-boat at
Versailles, a rowing-boat specially built
for Napoleon in 1811 and the *Belle Poule*
in which his remains were brought back
to France from the island of St Helena.
The *Gloire* dating from 1859 was the first
armoured warship in the world. And, of
course, exhibits includes ships used for
exploration, such as the *Astrolabe,* which
took Dumont d'Urville to the Antarctic
in the 19th century, and mementoes of
the great explorers La Pérouse, Brazza
and Charcot. Temporary exhibitions are
a regular feature.
*Place du Trocadéro, 75016. Tel: 45 53 31
70. Open: 10am–6pm. Closed: Tuesday.
Admission charge. Métro Trocadéro.*

MUSÉE MARMOTTAN

This is a strange museum which, as a
result of various bequests, has developed
from the original private collection into
an original museum of Impressionist
painting. It bears the name of the art
historian, Paul Marmottan, who, in
1932, donated his house and private
collections to the Académie des Beaux-
Arts. These included Renaissance
tapestries, furniture and sculpture as well
as early 19th-century paintings and *objets
d'art.*

Following other legacies, the museum
acquired some beautiful medieval
manuscripts and its first Impressionist
paintings, including Monet's famous
Impression (1872), which gave the
movement its name.

However, the outstanding asset of the
museum is the collection of 65 paintings
by Monet donated by his son in 1971.

Floating work of art, Musée de la Marine

Exhibited in a specially built
underground gallery, they testify to
Monet's love of his country home in
Giverny (see page 125). The different
moods of his garden are rendered with
supreme mastery. The studies of water-
lilies, for instance, show the master's
obsessive progression towards the huge
canvases exhibited in the Orangerie
museum (see page 94).
*2 rue Louis-Boilly, 75016. Tel: 42 24 07
02. Open: 10am–5.30pm. Closed:
Monday. Admission charge.
Métro La Muette.*

MUSÉE DE LA MONNAIE, see page 26

MUSÉE DES MONUMENTS FRANÇAIS

Housed in the east wing of the Palais de Chaillot, this museum was founded by the brilliant 19th-century architect, Viollet-le-Duc, who made such a splendid job of the restoration of Notre-Dame. He wanted to provide an opportunity to compare and study the evolution of monumental sculpture and architecture throughout France from the Romanesque period to the 19th century.

Grande Nu au Fauteuil Rouge –
Musée Picasso

It contains plaster casts of sculptures from outstanding French monuments as well as life-size replicas of parts of these monuments.
Place du Trocadéro, 75016. Tel: 47 27 35 74. Open: 9am–6pm. Closed: Tuesday. Admission charge. Métro Trocadéro.

Musée de Montmartre, see page 81
Musée National d'Art Moderne, see page 52
Musée Nissim de Camondo, see page 112

MUSÉE DE L'ORANGERIE

The south pavilion on the place de la Concorde, recently refurbished, houses a substantial collection of paintings from the Impressionist period to the early 20th century, but it is mostly renowned for Monet's *Nymphéas*. There are some remarkable still lifes by Cézanne, some delightful portraits by Renoir, and paintings by Picasso, Derain, Modigliani and Matisse, as well as a few of Henri Rousseau's best naïve works, including *La Carriole du Père Junier.*

Monet's huge *Nymphéas* (Water-lilies), painted at Giverny, are exhibited on the ground floor, in two oval rooms, according to the instructions of the artist.
Place de la Concorde, 75001. Tel: 42 97 48 16. Open: 9.45am–5.15pm. Closed: Tuesday. Admission charge. Métro Concorde.

Musée d'Orsay, see page 86
Musée du Petit Palais, see page 37

MUSÉE PICASSO

The ornate elegance of the 17th-century Hôtel Salé makes a perfect background for the works of a great master of 20th-century art. The building was renovated recently to accommodate a collection of Picasso's works donated to the state by his heirs in lieu of death duties: 200 paintings, more than 150 sculptures, 3,000 drawings and engravings, and 88 ceramics.

Picasso's personal collection of works by other major artists of his time, such as Cézanne, Derain, Braque, Miró, Rousseau and Matisse, was also donated to the state by Jacqueline Picasso.

Picasso's prodigious output is presented in a chronological order, starting on the first floor with the 'blue period' *(Autoportrait)*, followed by the Cubist period *(Nature morte à la chaise cannée)*. The period between World War I and World War II is illustrated by such paintings as *Paul en arlequin, le Baiser, Femme lisant* and the famous *Portrait de Dora Maar.* Among Picasso's post-war production, the series of studies on Manet's *Déjeuner sur l'Herbe* is particularly remarkable.

Some of Picasso's sculptures are exhibited in the garden, where there is also a pleasant café.
5 rue de Thorigny, 75003. Tel: 42 71 25 21. Open: 9.15am–5.15pm. Closed: Tuesday. Admission charge. Métro St-Paul.

Musée de la Poste, see page 85

MUSÉE RODIN

The superb collection of Rodin's sculptures is exhibited in the Hôtel Biron, where he lived from 1907 until his death in 1917. Some of his works, in bronze and white marble, are in the house while others are distributed round the beautiful garden, so that a visit to the museum on a sunny day is recommended.

In the garden are two of his most famous works: *Le Penseur* and *Les*

Bourgeois de Calais, as well as *La Porte de l'Enfer* and *Ugolin.* On the ground floor there are more masterpieces such as *Le Baiser* and *La Cathédrale.* On the first floor are the plaster casts used for the statues of Balzac and Victor Hugo.
77 rue de Varenne, 75007. Tel: 47 05 01 34. Open: 10am–5pm. Closed: Monday. Admission charge.
Métro Varenne.

Musée Seita, see page 112
Musée de la Serrure, see page 29
Musée du Vin, see page 113
Musée Zadkine, see page 85
Palais de la Découverte, see page 37
Pavillon de l'Arsenal, see page 45

Musée Rodin: works shown outdoors

Notre-Dame

*T*he harmonious strength of the cathedral's outline, the proportions of its façade, the subtle combination of simplicity and refinement in its design, are undoubtedly the perfect expression of French Gothic architecture. However, to Parisians and to the French people Notre-Dame is much more than that. It is the nucleus round which the capital developed and major celebrations, often marking a turning point in French history, were staged in there.

One of the cathedral's exquisite rose windows, a masterpiece within a masterpiece

Bishop Maurice de Sully

Bishop de Sully is particularly remembered among the thousands of anonymous stonemasons and artists who erected and decorated the cathedral because in 1163 he launched the building process that lasted nearly 200 years. The architects, Jean de Chelles and Pierre de Montreuil, worked on it during the 13th century, when the Ste-Chapelle was also built, and the building was completed in 1345 with the flying buttresses surrounding the chancel.

Notre-Dame today

Although the cathedral never suffered spectacular damage, by the mid-19th century it had been deprived of some of its magnificent sculptures and the edifice was in serious need of repair. Restoration work was carried out under the care of Viollet-Le-Duc, and the cathedral regained its past splendour. Haussmann later widened the Parvis (square) in front of it to increase the dramatic effect of its unique setting.

Today, two other vantage points, the square Jean XXIII behind the chancel and the square Viviani on the Left Bank, just across the Pont au Double, reveal the perfect proportions of the edifice, which is 130m long and 49m wide. Its twin towers rise to a height of 68m.

The façade

The façade is the most striking part of the building. The three portals are adorned with remarkable sculptures. The heavily restored central portal depicts the *Last Judgement*, and the upper part shows Christ surrounded by the celestial court. The portal of the Virgin on the left has a particularly beautiful tympanum illustrating the coronation of the Virgin Mary. The sculptures on the portal of St Anne on the right are the oldest in the cathedral; the remarkable tympanum again shows the Virgin Mary with Bishop Maurice de Sully, founder of the cathedral at her side. The lintel depicts scenes from the life of St Anne.

The rose window is over 700 years old. Birds and demons were placed at the base of the towers by Viollet-Le-Duc in true Gothic spirit. The great bell in the south tower, weighing 13 tons, is heard only on special occasions. The view from the top is rewarding if you have the courage to climb the 386 steps. The portal on the south side has a 13th-century tympanum, which depicts the martyr St Stephen. The slightly earlier north portal by Jean de Chelles was adorned with a statue of the Virgin and Child, but the child is now missing.

The interior

The vast interior can accommodate up to 9,000 people. The 35m high nave is separated from the chancel by a wide transept, which has two magnificent rose windows, the north rose having remained unaltered since the 13th century. The chancel was redecorated in the 17th century, as the result of a vow made by Louis XIII if he were granted an heir. A *pietà* by Coysevox stands in the centre, with statues of Louis XIII and XIV on either side. On the right of the chancel, the treasury houses some old manuscripts and relics, including a fragment of the Cross.

NOTRE-DAME	Towers – Open:
Place du Parvis de	10am–5pm.
Notre-Dame, 75004.	Admission charge.
Tel: 43 26 07 39.	
Open: 8am–7pm.	**Nearby:**
Métro St-Michel or	Ste-Chapelle
Cité, RER St-Michel-	Conciergerie
Notre-Dame.	Churches of
Treasury – Open:	St-Julien-le-Pauvre
10am–6pm,	and St-Séverin
Sunday from 2pm.	Musée de Cluny
Admission charge.	Ile St-Louis.

OPERA GARNIER

The architecture of this ornately decorated opera house epitomises the elaborate style of the 1860s. It was designed by Charles Garnier, a young and still unknown architect. He won the competition because of the boldness of his plans, which departed from the usual neoclassical style. When the Opéra was inaugurated in 1875, its vast stage, able to accommodate nearly 500 artists, ranked it among the world's finest opera houses and, for the last 100 years, it has welcomed the greatest international singers and dancers. Groups of statues by various artists welcome the spectators at the top of the steps, in front of the arcades marking the main entrance. One of them, *la Danse* by Carpeaux was considered highly immoral at the time; it has now been replaced by a copy and the original is in the Musée d'Orsay for safe keeping.

The interior is decorated with coloured marble; the grand staircase leads to the main foyer overlooking the

THE COMEDIE-FRANÇAISE

This famous theatre company was founded by Louis XIV in 1680, a few years after Molière's death, with the aim of combining two rival theatre companies. Frowned upon by the Sorbonne, it was forced to move several times, until Napoleon made it an official institution with a director appointed by the State. Its repertoire is traditionally classical, but also includes works by modern authors, both French and foreign. In the foyer is the chair that Molière collapsed into during a performance of *Le Malade Imaginaire*.

place de l'Opéra. In the auditorium, which seats around 2,000, red and gold are the dominant colours. The ceiling was painted by Chagall during the 1960s. The huge chandelier hanging in the centre weighs nearly 7 tons.
Place de l'Opéra, 75002. Tel: 47 42 53 71. Open: 11am–4.30pm. Closed: Sunday and when there is a performance. Métro Opéra.

PALAIS DE CHAILLOT

Ever since Catherine de Médicis had a country house built on the *colline de Chaillot* (Chaillot hill), the site has been sought after for its magnificent views of the river and the left bank.

In 1937, the present building was erected for the Exposition Universelle. Twin pavilions with curved wings are separated by a vast terrace beneath which is the Théâtre National de Chaillot, one of the leading French theatres (entrance through the east pavilion). The palace is large enough to house four museums, the Musée de l'Homme, Musée de la Marine, Musée des Monuments Français (see museums) and the Musée du Cinéma-Henri-Langlois. The latter depicts the history of motion pictures throughout the world, starting with Edison and the Lumière brothers. It includes models of studios, real sets and costumes worn by stars such as Valentino and Garbo.
Place du Trocadéro, 75016. Métro Trocadéro.
Musée du Cinéma – Open: daily except Tuesday, guided tours 10am, 11am, 2pm, 3pm and 4pm. Admission charge.

PALAIS-ROYAL

The palace was commissioned in 1624 by Richelieu, who was then Louis XIII's minister. It became a *palais royal* (royal palace) when he left it to the king in his

will. Louis XIV gave it to his brother, Philippe d'Orléans, whose descendants surrounded the garden with shopping arcades and apartments and built the Comédie-Française. Cafés, restaurants, gambling-houses and dance halls thrived within its precinct until, in the mid-19th century, Louis-Philippe took the fun out of the area by closing the gambling houses. The palace is not open to the public, but you can go through the main courtyard, invaded by the black and white Colonnes de Buren (pillars), into the peaceful garden surrounded by dainty boutiques.
Place du Palais-Royal. Métro Palais-Royal.

A series of pools fronts the Palais de Chaillot, across the river from the Eiffel Tower

PALAIS DE TOKYO

Situated a short distance up river from the Palais de Chaillot, the Palais de Tokyo was also built for the 1937 Exposition Universelle, in much the same style. The palace houses the Musée d'Art Moderne de la Ville de Paris (see page 88) and the surrounding terraces are decorated with statues by Emile Bourdelle.
11 avenue du Président-Wilson, 75016. Métro Alma-Marceau.

PANTHÉON

This vast monument towering over the Latin Quarter tends to dwarf everything around it, particularly the beautiful church of St-Etienne-du-Mont. Looked at from a distance, however, through the opening of the rue Soufflot, the harmonious proportions of its high dome, underlined by an elegant ring of slender columns, cannot fail to attract admiration for this splendid example of neoclassical architecture.

The Panthéon, where the illustrious rest

St Genevieve Church

When, in 1744, Louis XV suffered a serious illness, he vowed to build a beautiful new church to replace the ancient church of St Genevieve Abbey. After his recovery, he commissioned the architect, Soufflot, who designed a magnificent building in the shape of a Greek cross, with a huge dome 83m high; the saint's shrine would be placed beneath it. Work began in 1758, but was only completed after Soufflot's death in 1789, on the eve of the Revolution.

The Panthéon

In 1791, the Assemblée Constituante decided that all the nation's 'great men' should be buried inside the church, which was renamed Panthéon after the Greek and Roman temples dedicated to all the gods. However, with the return of the monarchy, the building became a church once again until, in 1885, the decision was finally taken to restore it to its role of national mausoleum, in honour of Victor Hugo who had just died.

The interior

Forty-two original windows were blocked up in 1791 and the bare walls were later decorated with scenes depicting the life of St Genevieve by Puvis de Chavannes and paintings by other late 19th-century artists. In the vast crypt are the tombs of some of France's 'great men': Voltaire, Rousseau, Hugo, Zola, the Resistance leader Jean Moulin, Jean Monnet, usually referred to as the 'father of Europe' and many others. As a symbolic gesture, President Mitterrand visited the Panthéon immediately after his election in 1981.

Place du Panthéon, 75005. Tel: 43 54 34

*51. Open: April to September 10am–noon,
2pm–6pm; October to May to 5pm).
Admission charge. Métro Cardinal-
Lemoine, RER Luxembourg.*

PLACE DES VOSGES

This beautiful square is a refreshing
haven compared to the magnificent place
de la Concorde or the supremely elegant
place Vendôme. Its sober yet extremely
refined architecture gives it a kind of
exquisite charm.

Commissioned by Henri IV at the
beginning of the 17th century, the
square was inaugurated after his death
by his son Louis XIII and named Place
Royale. The two higher buildings, in the
centre of the south and north sides, are
called respectively Pavillon du Roi
(King's Pavilion) and Pavillon de la
Reine (Queen's Pavilion), but were
never inhabited by the royal family. In
the central garden stands a statue of
Louis XIII. The square was renamed
Place des Vosges in 1800.

Some of the delightful residences
have been lived in by famous people:
Madame de Sévigné was born at no 1bis
in 1626, Cardinal Richelieu occupied no
21 before he moved to the Palais-Royal
and Victor Hugo lived in no 6 from 1832
to 1848, before his exile to Jersey and
Guernsey. The house is now a museum
with various mementoes of his life:
furniture, objects he collected, portraits
and photographs, but also drawings by
Hugo himself (see page 29).

*Musée Victor Hugo, 6 place des Vosges,
75004. Tel: 42 72 10 16. Open:
10am–5.40pm. Closed: Monday.
Admission charge. Métro St-Paul.*

PLACE VENDOME

Built at the end of the 17th century by
Jules Hardouin-Mansart, this imposing

Victor Hugo's house, place des Vosges

square is a magnificent example of the
Louis XIV style. Here again, symmetry
is the overriding principle: a terrace of
mansions over a row of arcades, with an
original feature designed to break the
monotony. The central buildings and
those cutting the four corners are
surmounted by pediments. Chopin died
at no 12 and no 15 is now the
prestigious Ritz Hotel; famous jewellers
are established all round the square.

The central column that replaced the
equestrian statue of Louis XIV was
erected by Napoleon to celebrate his
victory at Austerlitz. The statue at the
top was changed many times until the
Third Republic finally settled on a copy
of the original representing Napoleon in
Roman dress (see page 33).

Métro Concorde or Opéra.

LES QUAIS

The quais (embankment) are the city's main thoroughfares, carrying fast-moving traffic from east to west and vice versa. Lined with wide pavements planted with trees, the quais offer lovely walks along the river with fine views of the monuments sited on both banks of the Seine and on the Ile-de-la-Cité: the Louvre, the Musée d'Orsay, the Conciergerie, the Hôtel de Ville and Notre-Dame, to name but a few.

The Right Bank

The quai de la Mégisserie and the quai de Gesvres are lined with picturesque pet shops. From here there is a splendid view across the river of the Conciergerie on the Ile-de-la-Cité. The tiny square de l'Ave Maria offers an interesting view of the medieval Hôtel de Sens. Across the Pont Marie is the peaceful Ile St-Louis.

The Left Bank

There are striking views of Notre-Dame from the quai de la Tournelle, and from the quai de Montebello; just off the latter is the delightful square René-

Used books: Shakespeare & Co, Left Bank

LES BOUQUINISTES

Second-hand bookstalls are one of the familiar sights of Paris, and a stroll along the river would be less enjoyable without them. The tattered, green-painted boxes that used to be carried to and fro by their owners have become permanent fixtures. At night they are closed and padlocked, but in the afternoon they open one by one, like stranded sea shells, revealing books, prints, postcards and maps. A good browse under their precariously propped-up lids is always fun, although there are not many rare editions or bargains to be found anymore!

Viviani. Past the place St-Michel, the quai des Grands-Augustins, named after a nearby monastery, is lined with second-hand bookstalls on the river side and with a couple of 17th-century mansions on the other side. The Pont-Neuf, the oldest bridge in Paris, is in two sections and joins the Right and Left banks to the Ile-de-la-Cité.
Métro Pont-Neuf, Châtelet, Pont-Marie and St-Michel.

SACRE-COEUR

Visible from almost anywhere in Paris, the white basilica has become one of the city's most famous landmarks. The decision to build it was taken by the Assemblée Nationale in 1873, to boost the public's morale after the Franco-Prussian War. Work got underway in 1875, but the building was only completed in 1914 and consecrated after World War I. Its architecture is, to say the least, disappointing, but its Byzantine style makes it instantly recognisable on the Paris skyline. The mosaic decorating the chancel vaulting is impressive, and it is possible to go up to the top of the dome for a superb panoramic view of Paris.

Parvis du Sacré-Coeur, 75018. Tel: 42 51 17 02. Métro Anvers, then access by funicular.
Dome: 9.15am–7pm. Admission charge.

STE-CHAPELLE

A slender spire rising into the sky reveals from a distance the presence of this jewel of Gothic architecture, partly hidden by the Palais de Justice buildings. In 1239, Louis IX, better known as St-Louis, acquired the Crown of Thorns from the Emperor of Constantinople, together with other precious relics including a fragment of the True Cross, and immediately decided to build a special shrine to house them in the courtyard of the royal palace. Pierre de Montreuil was entrusted with this delicate task. The Ste-Chapelle was built in less than three years and consecrated in 1248. After the Revolution, it was no longer used as a church and the relics were transferred to Notre-Dame where they are now kept in the Treasury.

Sacré-Coeur, rich in Romanesque detail

A glittering shrine

In order to let in as much light as possible, the vaulted roof was supported by thin pillars separated by long, narrow stained-glass windows 15m high. A few buttresses help to reinforce the structure, which appears to have no walls. The distinctive 75m high spire can be spotted from afar. The narrow edifice consists of two superposed chapels, one above the other.

The *chapelle basse* (lower chapel) is only 7m high. It is richly decorated and its floor is paved with tombstones. A spiral staircase gives access to the *chapelle haute* (upper chapel) which appears wrapped in a blaze of light and colour. The huge stained-glass windows are the most striking feature: still mainly 13th-century, they are the oldest in Paris. Over 1,000 scenes from the Old and New Testaments, depicted in great detail and warm, bright colours, unfold all the way round like a pictorial Bible.

4 boulevard du Palais, 75004. Tel: 43 54 30 09. Open: 9.30am–6.30pm (summer), 10am–5pm (winter). Admission charge. Access through the Cour de Mai of the Palais de Justice. Métro St-Michel or Cité.

Les Deux Magots, a café frequented by post-war philosophers and poets like Jean-Paul Sartre

ST-GERMAIN-DES-PRÉS

Situated on the Left Bank, next to the Latin Quarter, St-Germain-des-Prés has, since the days of Jean-Paul Sartre and the Existentialists, been known as the rallying place of the intellectual avant-garde, who traditionally met in the literary cafés of the boulevard St-Germain. The district nestles round the ancient church of St-Germain des Prés (see page 55) and abounds in interesting contrasts. The wide boulevard St-Germain, cutting right across it and carrying fast traffic eastwards, is noisy and dusty and rather spoils the immediate surroundings of the church, but the back streets are delightful, each having its own attractive feature. There is the rue de Buci with its lively open-air market and the very old streets in the vicinity of the quaint place de Fürstemberg, rue Cardinale, rue de l'Echaudé going back to the 14th century and rue Bourbon-le-Château.

Further west, rue Bonaparte and rue des Sts-Pères, running down to the river, are lined with old-fashioned antique shops and art galleries while rue Jacob, at right-angles to them, is one of the most pleasant streets in the area. On the busy boulevard St-Germain, near the place St-Germain-des-Prés, are the well-known cafés closely associated with the district, the Café des Deux Magots and the Café de Flore.

Métro St-Germain-des-Prés or Mabillon.

STE-MARIE MADELEINE

This church in the guise of a Greek temple is known to Parisians simply as La Madeleine. Two partly erected churches were successively razed before Napoleon had this temple built in honour of his Grande Armée. It was completed only in 1842 and by then it had been decided that the temple would be a church. Fifty-two massive Corinthian columns surround the building which dominates the centre of the place de la Madeleine with its flower-market and well-known luxury delicatessens, Hédiard and Fauchon. Inside the church are some interesting 19th-century sculptures including *Le Baptême du Christ* by François Rude and *Le Mariage de la Vierge* by Pradier. *Place de la Madeleine, 75008. Tel: 42 65 52 17. Métro Madeleine.*

The jewel-like beauty of Ste-Chapelle

Tête-à-tête, boulevard St-Germain

LITERARY CAFÉS

Several cafés near the church of St-Germain des Prés have at different times been the rendezvous of intellectuals and artists. The Procope, rue de l'Ancienne-Comédie, just off the carrefour de l'Odéon, is the oldest. It was opened in 1686 by a Sicilian called Francesco Procopio, who made such good coffee, that his establishment soon became the meeting-place of actors from the Comédie-Française opposite; later of philosophers such as Voltaire and Rousseau, revolutionaries like Danton, Robespierre and Marat and famous 19th-century writers and poets, Musset, George Sand, Balzac and Hugo. The claim to fame of the Flore and the Deux Magots is much more recent. In the late 1940s and 1950s, they became the favourite haunt of Sartre, Simone de Beauvoir, Camus, Prévert and the whole post-war generation of philosophers and poets. They are still favoured by today's intellectuals, but the magic has gone.

Streets and Squares

*E*legant streets and popular ones, imposing squares and tiny, quaint ones, all reflect the life of the city, in turn quiet and bustling, hurried and leisurely.

Rue Mouffetard, which charmed Hemingway with its old houses and shopfronts of character

Rue Mouffetard

Running downhill from the top of the Montagne Ste-Geneviève, the rue Mouffetard is one of the most picturesque streets in Paris. The bottom section is the liveliest, with its open-air market, the colourful shop signs creating a village-like atmosphere. A little way up, on either side, are the passage des Postes and the passage des Patriarches, both worth exploring, while further up still,

on the left, the rue du Pot-de-Fer has some interesting restaurants. The Fontaine du Pot-de-Fer, on the corner, was built in the 17th century and supplied by an aqueduct that brought water to the Palais du Luxembourg. The street ends at the charming place de la Contrescarpe.
75005. Métro Monge or Censier-Daubenton.

Rue Quincampoix

Situated near the Centre Pompidou, this old street was the scene in 1720 of a famous scandal involving the Scottish

financier, John Law. He founded a bank that encouraged wild speculation and the inevitable crash ruined thousands. There are some interesting old houses near the junction with rue des Lombards.
75004. Métro Châtelet or Rambuteau.

Rue Royale

This elegant street, which links the place de la Concorde and the Madeleine, has wide pavements lined with luxury shops. Near the place de la Concorde, Maxim's is still one of the leading restaurants of the capital.
75008. Métro Concorde or Madeleine.

Rue St-André-des-Arts

Going west towards St-Germain-des-Prés from the Latin Quarter, the rue St-André-des-Arts is popular with young people and tourists enjoying the incessant animation around the cafés, crêperies, snack bars, souvenir shops and book shops. The Cour du Commerce St-André on the left is an 18th-century arcade lined with shops and cafés with picturesque old beams.
75006. Métro St-Michel.

Place du Châtelet

This was extensively remodelled by Haussmann, who commissioned two theatres from the architect Davioud: the Théâtre du Châtelet, where musicals, operas and concerts are still regularly staged, and the Théâtre de la Ville, once the Théâtre Sarah Bernhardt, where the famous actress delighted Parisians with her inspired performances.
75001. Métro Châtelet.

Place Emile-Goudeau

This unpretentious square, where the famous Bateau Lavoir building (see page 83) once stood, still possesses some of the old magic of Montmartre.
75018. Métro Abbesses.

Place de l'Odéon

The square has hardly altered since the late 18th century. The sober architecture of its houses contrasts with the Greek-temple style of the Théâtre National de l'Odéon dating from 1782. The Café Voltaire at no 1 used to be the meeting place of 18th-century philosophers, including Voltaire, Diderot and D'Alembert.
75006. Métro Odéon.

Meridian Line, St-Sulpice

Place St-Sulpice

Dominated by its monumental fountain (see page 65) and the twin-towered church of St-Sulpice (see page 57), this square is an ideal place for a pause while visiting the St-Germain-des-Prés area.
75006. Métro St-Sulpice or Mabillon.

Place des Victoires

The original statue of Louis XIV was installed by a rich admirer of the king who subsequently had the square designed by Mansart to match the statue. Recently renovated, the square has attracted several well-known fashion boutiques.
75002. Métro Bourse or Palais-Royal.

Tour Eiffel
(Eiffel Tower)

*I*ts spindly greyish figure has been painted, photographed, joked about, written and sung about more than any other monument in Paris and today, after more than 100 years, it still retains the key to its initial success: instant appeal. Once your curiosity is roused, it will continue to grow as you get closer, and you will never be disappointed for it is a strange monument indeed, with its graceful outline, combined with the huge steel struts that are locked together in an intricate web.

Scientific and artistic challenge

It is no surprise that the idea of such a daring project should have come from a group of engineers headed by Gustave Eiffel, working on steel bridges and viaducts. Plans submitted by Maurice Koechlin and Emile Nouguier won first prize in a competition organised for the 1889 Exposition Universelle and Gustave Eiffel exclaimed enthusiastically: 'France will be the only nation with a 300m flagstaff!'.

Queuing to climb the 1,710 steps to the top

Built in record time

The tower was completed by 300 workers in just over two years from January 1887 to March 1889. This was made possible by the extreme precision of the plans, which gave the exact measurements for over 12,000 metallic parts.Two and a half million rivets were used and, when it was inaugurated, it was the tallest building in the world.

VITAL STATISTICS

Total height: 320m
First floor: 57m
Second floor: 115m
Third floor: 276m
1,710 steps to the top
Weight: 7,000 tons
Maximum sway at the top: 12cm
40 tons of paint are needed to repaint it every seven years.
It has 4 million visitors a year.

For and against

The tower's success was immediate. During the six months of the exhibition, nearly 2 million visitors came to see the 'iron lady' and, by the end of the year, three-quarters of the building cost had already been recovered. The tower may have had its fans, but it also had its critics. Three hundred writers and artists signed a protest addressed to the municipality, qualifying it as 'useless and monstrous'.

Champ de Mars,

75007.

Tel: 45 50 34 56.

Open: 10am–11pm.

Admission charge.

Métro Trocadéro or

Bir-Hakeim, RER

Champ-de-Mars-

Tour-Eiffel.

Nearby:

Jardins du Trocadéro

Palais de Chaillot and

its museums

Musée des Arts

Asiatiques-Guimet

Musée d'Art Moderne

de la Ville de Paris.

Once vilified on aesthetic grounds, now a favourite subject of artists

A narrow escape

The concession had been granted for 20 years only and the tower, which had always been considered as temporary, was due to be pulled down in 1909. However, by then it was playing an essential role in the rapidly developing world of telecommunications. It was saved, and proved to be an indispensable asset in establishing the first radio telephone service across the Atlantic, for instance, and as a meteorological station. In 1957, its height increased by another 20m when a television transmitter was fitted at the top. In preparation for its hundredth anniversary, it was completely repainted and glitters now under more powerful lights.

The climb!

A visit to the viewing platforms is a must for anyone who comes to Paris for the first time, as the view from the top floor is breath-taking, and can extend 67km in exceptional weather conditions. Try and chose a clear day and wait until late afternoon, when the sun has had time to disperse all signs of morning mist. Of course, you will most probably have to queue for the lifts as the tower is very popular. On your way up, you may wish to stop on the first floor where there is a free video show on the history of the building. There are also snack bars for refreshment.

Millions of skeletons lie in the Catacombs

UNKNOWN PARIS

There are aspects of Parisian life that have nothing in common with the breathtaking vistas, impressive monuments or glamour associated with the Champs-Elysées-Madeleine-Opéra districts. You can stroll along the Canal St-Martin, meditate in the Père Lachaise cemetery, discover a hidden arcade or an unusual little museum or just watch Parisians getting on with their daily life.

UNDERGROUND PARIS

The city's network of tunnels has many practical uses other than the métro, and part of it can be visited.

In the 18th century, Parisians found a new use for some underground galleries on the site of Roman stone quarries. They became a much-needed cemetery to relieve the overcrowded Cimetière des Innocents, situated near les Halles, where the Fontaine des Innocents now stands. The site was consecrated and the bones were piled along the galleries. There are now guided visits to these 'catacombs'.

Les Catacombes, 1 place Denfert-Rochereau, 75014. Tel: 43 22 47 63. Open: 2pm–4pm, also 9am–11am on Saturdays and Sundays. Closed: Monday. Admission charge. Métro Denfert-Rochereau.

Les Egouts (sewers) formed part of the modernisation programme of Baron Haussmann in the 19th century, the network totalling some 2,000km. The visit includes the showing of a video film which explains how the whole system works.

Place de la Résistance, 75007. Tel: 47 05 10 29. Open: 11am–4pm. Closed: Thursday and Friday. Admission charge. Métro Alma-Marceau.

Along the Canal St-Martin

The canal St-Martin was dug in the early 19th century to link the canal de l'Ourcq, running eastwards from La Villette, and the Seine. It winds its way across the eastern districts of Paris over a distance of 4.5km and joins the river just south of the Bastille.

The most picturesque section lies between rue du Faubourg du Temple and rue Louis Blanc. The most relaxing way to enjoy the canal is to take a three-hour cruise from the Musée d'Orsay to La Villette. (For more information see the **Practical Guide**, Organised Tours.)

For those who prefer to walk beside the canal, the best way is to start either from the place de la République (métro République) or the place de Stalingrad (métro Stalingrad or Jaurès).

Arcades

Covered arcades were in fashion at the end of the 18th and at the beginning of the 19th century. Some of them, like the Galerie Vivienne, were elaborately decorated. Called *galeries* or *passages,* they are today often lined with unusual picturesque boutiques. The most interesting ones are situated between rue de Rivoli and the Grands Boulevards, west of the boulevard de Sébastopol. The following should not be missed:

Galerie Vivienne, 4 rue des Petits-Champs, 75002. Métro Bourse.
Passage Choiseul, 23 rue St-Augustin, 75002. Métro Quatre-Septembre.
Passage des Princes, 97 rue de Richelieu, 75002. Métro Richelieu-Drouot.
Passage des Panoramas, 11 boulevard Montmartre.
Passage Jouffroy, 12 boulevard Montmartre.
Passage Verdeau, 31 bis rue du Faubourg-Montmartre, 75009. Metro le Peletier.
Passage du Caire, 2 place du Caire, 75002. Métro Sentier.
Galerie Véro-Dodat, 19 rue Jean-Jacques Rousseau, 75001. Métro Louvre-Rivoli.

Cimetière du Père-Lachaise

This is Paris's largest cemetery. A plan is available at the main entrance to help you locate the graves of the famous: Alfred de Musset who was buried beneath a weeping willow, the tragic

lovers Héloïse and Abélard, Oscar Wilde, Molière, Hugo, Baron Haussmann, Sarah Bernhardt, Edith Piaf and a host of others.
Main entrance boulevard de Ménilmontant, 75020. Métro Père-Lachaise.

On the east side of the cemetery is the old village of Charonne. Its medieval church of St-Germain-de-Charonne is surrounded by a tiny cemetery, and its high street, rue St-Blaise, is lined with small houses. The area has managed to retain its village atmosphere despite being close to the high-rise buildings of Belleville and Ménilmontant, north of the Père Lachaise.
Métro Gambetta.

Musée des Arts et Traditions Populaires

Situated in the Bois de Boulogne, this museum depicts aspects of French society through its traditions and daily life in rural areas, including folk art, local customs and games.
6 avenue du Mahatma Gandhi, 75016. Tel: 40 67 90 00. Open: 9.45am–5.15pm. Closed: Tuesday. Admission charge. Métro Les Sablons.

Musée Cernuschi

The house and personal collection of Oriental art of the banker Henri Cernuschi form the basis of this museum, bequeathed to the city of Paris before his death in 1896. Ancient Chinese art, including Neolithic terracottas, is particularly well represented.
7 avenue Vélasquez, 75008. Tel: 45 63 50 75. Open: 10am–5.40pm. Closed: Monday. Admission charge. Métro Monceau or Villiers.

Left: Piaf's tomb, Père Lachaise cemetery

The Musée Seita is devoted to tobacco and its associated artefacts and rituals

UNKNOWN PARIS
Musée des Lunettes et des Lorgnettes

The history of spectacles and various kinds of glasses, such as opera and field-glasses, is depicted by means of many fascinating exhibits, sometimes elaborately decorated.
2 avenue Mozart, 75016. Tel: 45 27 21 05. Open: Monday 10.30am–noon and 2pm–6pm, Tuesday to Friday 9.30am–6pm. Closed: Saturday and Sunday. Métro La Muette.

Musée Nissim de Camondo

This private mansion backing on to the parc Monceau was donated to the nation by the Comte de Camondo. It re-creates the interior of an elegant 18th-century house with furniture made by the most famous cabinet-makers, Beauvais tap-estries, precious ornaments and china.
63 rue Monceau, 75008. Tel: 45 63 26 32. Open: 10am–noon and 2pm–5pm. Closed: Monday and Tuesday. Admission charge. Métro Villiers or Monceau.

Musée Seita

This is an unusual museum depicting the development of smoking customs since Jean Nicot imported tobacco into France in the 16th century and unknowingly gave his name to one of its harmful ingredients, nicotine.
Exhibits include numerous pipes, snuffboxes, cigarette cases and shop signs.
12 rue Surcouf, 75007. Tel: 45 56 60 17. Open: 11am–6pm, Closed: Sunday. Admission charge. Métro Invalides.

NOUVELLE ATHENES

Situated south of the place Pigalle, this district owes its romantic name partly to the neoclassical architecture of its houses and partly to the fact that, in the 1830s, it attracted the artistic and intellectual elite of the capital and rivalled the Faubourg St-Germain.

The **Musée de la Vie Romantique,** housed in the former home of the painter Ary Scheffer, is devoted to the artists and writers who used to be his regular guests: George Sand, Chopin, Delacroix, Liszt, Dickens, Turgenev and many others.
16 rue Chaptal, 75009. Tel: 48 74 95 38. Open: 10am–5.40pm. Closed: Monday. Admission charge. Métro St-Georges or Pigalle.

Another 19th-century painter's house, close by in rue de la Rochefoucauld, has been turned into a museum: the **Musée Gustave Moreau.** Moreau's symbolism influenced his famous pupils, Rouault and Matisse.
14 rue de la Rochefoucauld, 75009. Tel: 48 74 38 50. Open: Wednesday 11am–5.15pm, other days 10am–12.45pm and 2pm–5.45pm. Closed: Monday and Tuesday. Admission charge. Métro Trinité or St-Georges.

PASSY
Annexed to the city of Paris in 1860, the 'village' of Passy is today a sought-after residential district in the western part of the capital.

The **Maison de Balzac** is a museum devoted to the 19th-century novelist who depicted French society with such mastery. It contains manuscripts, caricatures and engravings. Balzac lived in the house for seven years and regularly evaded his creditors by slipping out through the back entrance in the cobbled rue Berton.
47 rue Raynouard, 75016. Tel: 42 24 56

38. Open: 10am–5.40. Closed: Monday. Admission charge. Métro Passy or RER Kennedy-Radio-France.

The **Musée du Vin** has found an appropriate home in the ancient cellars of the 14th-century former Abbey of Passy; it illustrates the history of wine-making and wine-tasting is included in the visit.
Rue des Eaux, 75016. Tel: 45 25 63 26. Open: noon–6pm. Admission charge. Métro Passy.

TEMPLE
This district south of the place de la République was named after the Knights Templar. In 1808 the site was turned into an open-air second-hand clothes market known as the Carreau du Temple because the clothes were laid directly on the pavement. Today, cheap clothes are sold in a covered market, but the site has retained its picturesque name.
Métro Temple.

VAL-DE-GRÂCE
The buildings of the former abbey are situated on the edge of the Latin Quarter. Mansart designed the church in the Jesuit style fashionable at the time, with a two-tier façade, a dome modelled on St Peter's in Rome and above all superb baroque decorations. Particularly remarkable are the huge baldachin resting on six twisted columns, and the painting in the cupola by Pierre Mignard, which includes a great number of gigantic figures. Following the Revolution, the abbey became a military hospital.
Rue St-Jacques (boulevard de Port-Royal end), 75005. RER Port-Royal or Luxembourg.

La Villette

*T*he vast complex of La Villette is still under development on both sides of the canal de l'Ourcq, between the Porte de la Villette and the Porte de Pantin. Buildings on the original site have been incorporated into the project, which includes the Cité des Sciences et de l'Industrie (a science and technology complex), the Cité de la Musique (a music complex) and various other cultural facilities, as well as a park with a choice of leisure activities, spread over an area of 55 hectares. The object of building a major new cultural centre on the edge of the city was to revive interest in this long-neglected eastern district, while taking advantage of the enormous amount of space available.

CITÉ DES SCIENCES ET DE L'INDUSTRIE

Inaugurated in 1986, it has already proved very successful, attracting an increasing number of visitors of all ages. Much more than a museum, it is a constantly updated reference centre, keeping track of the rapid evolution of

The spectacular Géode is set in a landscaped park with good family facilities

science and technology. Its novelty lies in the fact that the public is encouraged to take part in various projects and demonstrations. This makes it a realistic and entertaining study centre, particularly suitable for children.

The building itself, incorporating a former 19th-century auction hall, was designed by Fainsilber, who used the reflection of light off the steel-and-glass structure to achieve futuristic effects.

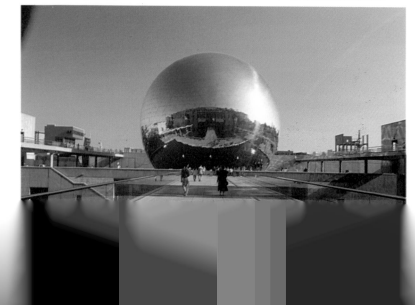

The glass reveals mechanisms usually kept hidden, as in the main escalators or the glasshouses on the south façade.

EXPLORA

This permanent exhibition, staged on three levels and including tours, activities and workshops, illustrates four broad themes.

'The earth and the universe' deals with the exploration of the oceans, the geological history of the earth, movements of the continents, travel and experiments in space. The planetarium aims to explain the complexity of the universe with programmes such as 'Life and death of a star' and 'Space oasis'. 'The adventure of life' deals with the human environment, man and the secrets of life. 'Man and matter' is concerned with man's control of energy and other resources, transport and economic trends. 'Language and communications' covers the world of sounds and images and various aspects of man's social behaviour.

The centre also includes a fully computerised, multi-media library with special material available for children *(la médiathèque)*, a cinema showing documentaries and fiction films to introduce viewers to the world of science *(le cinéma Louis-Lumière)*, and two discovery areas for children aged 3 to 6 and 6 to 12 *(l'inventorium)*.

LA GÉODE

This shiny steel globe, close to the main building, acts as a vast mirror, reflecting the surroundings and the changing sky with great intensity.

The auditorium has a 1,000sq m hemispheric screen. Films on scientific subjects are shown throughout the day.

The Maison de la Villette, housed in the recently renovated Rotonde des Vétérinaires, has an exhibition of local history.

The park extends across the canal de l'Ourcq: green open spaces, with red *folies* (follies) dotted about. These are see-through cubical pavilions, varying in shape and used for practical purposes. There is a children's centre, information centre, video studios, café and first aid centre.

The Grande Halle, dating from 1867, is an iron structure that served as a cattle market until the 1970s. It is now an ideal venue for exhibitions and trade fairs.

The Zénith is a vast hall that can accommodate some 6,500 spectators and is used mainly for rock concerts.

The Cité de la Musique, which is the other main complex in the park, is not fully operational yet. It is already the home of the Conservatoire National Supérieur de Musique, the higher national music academy, and will eventually house a concert hall and a museum of musical instruments.

Cité des Sciences et de l'Industrie, 30 avenue Corentin-Cariou, 75019. Tel: 46 42 13 13. Open: 10am–6pm. Closed: Monday. Admission charge; headsets for self-guided audiotour of Explora in English can be rented.

Métro Porte-de-la-Villette or Corentin-Cariou. La Géode: film shows every hour from 10am–9pm. Admission charge. Cité de la Musique, avenue Jean-Jaurès, 75019. Métro Porte de Pantin (work still in progress).

Paris environs

LA DEFENSE

This entirely modern district lies to the west of Paris, across the Pont de Neuilly. A statue in the central square, symbolising the defence of Paris during the Franco-Prussian war of 1871, gives the area its name.

Bold town planning

Town planners had been toying for a long time with the idea of extending the Voie Triomphale designed by Le Nôtre in the 17th century, which sweeps across the city in a straight line from the Louvre to the Arc de Triomphe. Development began in the late 1950s, and architects experimented with new ideas. One of the driving principles was the total separation of pedestrian and motorised traffic. The vast complex is surrounded by a *boulevard circulaire* (ringroad) carrying through traffic, with underground link roads and outlets leading to specific areas at different levels. A broad pedestrian avenue, called the Esplanade du Général de Gaulle, rises in steps from the Seine and gives access to the various groups of buildings: a variety of towers housing offices, a few blocks of flats, a vast shopping complex called Les Quatre-Temps and the CNIT (Centre National des Industries et des Techniques), the oldest building on the site. Its concrete shell, resting on just three supports, was considered revolutionary in 1958! It has recently been converted into an international business centre.

La Grande Arche

Inaugurated in 1989 for the bicentenary of the Revolution, the arch was the last project to be built.

Designed by the Danish architect, Otto von Spreckelsen, the arch is shaped like a huge hollow cube, and is faced with glass and white Carrara marble. It is slightly out of alignment with the axis of the Voie Triomphale. The arch is so vast in fact that Notre-Dame (spire included) would fit beneath it!

The complex glass and steel structure of the external lifts offsets the extreme simplicity of the outline and the *nuages* (clouds) suspended below the arch add a whimsical touch. The lifts take visitors up to the roof (le Belvédère) to admire the beautiful views over Paris.

3.5km west of the Porte Maillot, RER La Défense; the métro is being extended from the Pont de Neuilly.

MALMAISON

Situated 10km west of Paris, the 17th-century Château de Malmaison is famous for its connection with Napoleon. His first wife, Joséphine de Beauharnais, bought the castle in 1799, and Napoleon always loved the place. After their divorce, Josephine kept Malmaison for a short while until her premature death in 1814. When he escaped from the island of Elba and returned to France, Napoleon went to Malmaison to recall happy memories, and again just before he was finally exiled on the island of St Helena.

The castle had many owners before it was eventually donated to the nation and turned into a museum, housing mementoes of Napoleon and Joséphine. Some of the original furniture from their various residences is on display.

Musée National du Château de

The cavernous Grande Arch, La Défense, has a rooftop exhibition gallery

Malmaison, avenue du Château, 92500 Rueil-Malmaison. Tel: 47 49 20 07. Open: 10am–noon; 1.30pm–5pm. Closed: Tuesday. Admission charge. RER Rueil-Malmaison.

The nearby Château de Bois-Préau, which also belonged to Joséphine, is devoted to mementoes of Napoleon's stay on the island of St Helena. The two museums are linked.
Avenue de l'Impératrice Joséphine, 92500 Rueil-Malmaison. Open: 10.30am–12.30pm; 1.30pm–5pm. Closed: Tuesday.

SEVRES

This small town, 10km west of Paris, has become synonymous with beautiful china. The Manufacture Nationale de Porcelaine began making fine porcelain here in the 18th century. Its specialities include the famous *bleu de Sèvres,* a deep blue on a pure white background, and exquisite *biscuits,* unglazed delicate statuettes.

Founded in 1824, the Musée National de la Céramique contains precious exhibits from all over the world. *Place de la Manufacture, 92310 Sèvres. Tel: 45 34 99 05. Open: 10am–5.15pm. Closed: Tuesday. Admission charge. Métro Pont de Sèvres.*

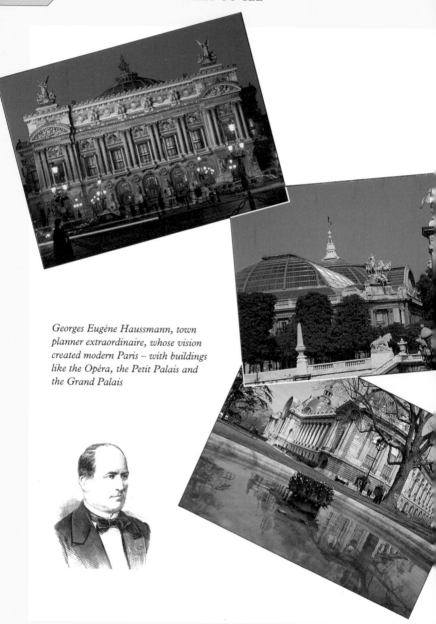

Georges Eugène Haussmann, town planner extraordinaire, whose vision created modern Paris – with buildings like the Opéra, the Petit Palais and the Grand Palais

Baron Haussmann's
Revolution

Just over 100 years ago, a revolution shook Paris to its very foundations and altered the city more drastically than 1789 had done. It was orchestrated by one man, Baron Haussmann, with the enthusiastic approval of Napoleon III.

By 1850, the town had grown round its medieval centre without any coherence, and the squalid, narrow streets were a constant health hazard. Moreover, growing social problems threatened the fragile political stability.

From 1853 to 1870, Haussmann's engineers and architects cut right through the heart of the old city, laying waste whole districts, installing an adequate water supply and a network of sewers, creating wide avenues and building rows and rows of six-storey blocks of flats which have become one of the familiar sights of the town.

Modern Paris emerged out of the chaos and soon became known as *la ville lumière,* an harmonious ensemble of green open spaces, including the Bois de Boulogne, of spacious tree-lined boulevards and imposing public buildings such as the Opéra.

Haussmann's far-seeing town planning was conceived on a scale that left room for expansion and by the end of the century the railway stations, the Eiffel Tower, and the Grand and the Petit Palais had all taken their rightful place on the Paris scene.

The painful surgery Haussmann imposed on the capital was, however, much criticised at the time by such public figures as Victor Hugo, George Sand and Alexandre Dumas, who denounced the ruthless break with the past and the crippling cost of these 'extravagant' schemes, which encouraged speculation.

But history has passed a more favourable judgement for it was Haussmann who enabled Paris to blossom into the unique capital city it is today.

ST-DENIS

This industrialised northern suburb is famous for its beautiful Gothic cathedral, where most French monarchs have traditionally been buried.

The legend of St-Denis

The first bishop of Paris, Saint-Denis, martyred in Montmartre, is said to have walked, holding his head in his hands, to a field where he died and was buried. His grave soon became a place of pilgrimage and the first church was built there in the 5th century; then, in 630, King Dagobert founded a powerful abbey to control the growing numbers of pilgrims. He was buried in the new church, which became the traditional burial place of his successors.

The Gothic church

Abbot Suger is closely linked to the history of the present cathedral. Born of poor parents, he was taken into care by the abbey. His exceptional gifts having won him the confidence of Louis VII, he became abbot of St-Denis in 1122 and designed a great Gothic cathedral, which served as a prototype for later masterpieces such as Chartres Cathedral. The edifice was completed in just over 10 years. During the second half of the 13th century, Saint-Louis had the nave and transept rebuilt by Pierre de Montreuil, the architect of the Ste-Chapelle, but the beautiful façade remained unaltered.

Grossly neglected over the centuries, the cathedral suffered great damage during the 1789 Revolution. Restoration work carried out in the 19th century involved the pulling down of the north tower. Viollet-le-Duc, who also restored Notre-Dame, finally undertook to save what was left.

Bearly friends at the Bois de Vincennes

The cathedral today

The façade looks mutilated without its north tower. The base of the towers, over the rose window, is crenellated, a reminder that the edifice was originally fortified. The tympanum of the main portal illustrates the *Last Judgement,* the other two being connected with Saint-Denis.

The cathedral is, above all, a museum of the French monarchy, with its numerous funeral monuments carved by the greatest sculptors. In the 13th century, Saint-Louis commissioned monuments for his predecessors, the most remarkable being Dagobert's imposing tomb. It became the tradition for later kings to have their own grave designed. Some, dating from the Renaissance, are particularly elaborate, such as the monument commissioned by Catherine de Médicis for herself and Henri II.

In the Romanesque crypt is the collective grave of all the Bourbons.
Place de l'Hôtel de Ville, 93200 St-Denis. Tel: 48 09 83 54. Open: 10am–5pm, 7pm in summer. Métro St-Denis-Basilique.

VINCENNES

The Château and Bois de Vincennes lie just beyond the périphérique, on the eastern side of Paris.

The Château

Situated on the edge of what was once royal hunting ground, the Château de Vincennes dates from the 14th century. During the reign of Louis XIV, pavilions were built on either side of the courtyard overlooking the forest by the architect Le Vau. By then the keep had become a state prison, Fouquet and Mirabeau being among its unwilling guests. Extensive work has now restored the castle as it was in the 17th century.

Near the entrance, the Tour du Village, which formed part of the fortified wall, is the only one to have retained its original height of 42m. The imposing keep, 52m high, is surrounded by a separate wall and moat. It houses a museum depicting the castle's history. Henry V of England died in the royal chamber on the second floor.
Avenue de Paris, 94300 Vincennes. Tel: 43 28 15 48. Open: 10am–4.15pm, 6.15pm in summer. Admission charge. Métro Château de Vincennes.

The Bois de Vincennes

This has been known to generations of French schoolchildren as the place where Saint-Louis used to administer justice seated under an oak tree. In 1860 Haussmann remodelled it into an English style park, with lakes and a racecourse. The Parc Floral de Paris, a flower garden covering 30 hectares, and a zoo, are also situated here.
Parc Floral de Paris – route de la Pyramide. Open: 9.30am–5pm. Admission charge. Métro Château de Vincennes.
Parc zoologique – avenue Daumesnil. Open: 9am–5.30pm. Admission charge. Métro Porte Dorée.

Right: The Ste-Chapelle in the grounds of Vincennes

Musée des Arts d'Afrique et d'Océanie

Among the most interesting exhibits of this museum are a collection of painted bark from Australia, masks from Africa and fine samples of North African crafts.
293 avenue Daumesnil. Tel: 43 43 14 54. Open: 10am–noon and 1.30pm–5.30pm. Closed: Tuesday. Admission charge. Métro Porte Dorée.

Excursions

Chartres Cathedral, magnet for pilgrims, displays the Virgin's tunic in the Treasury

CHANTILLY

Situated north of Paris on the edge of an ancient forest, in the heart of horse-racing country, the Château de Chantilly is surrounded by a beautiful park with ponds and lakes.

The castle

The history of the castle goes back to Roman times, Cantilius was the first nobleman to build a fortified house on the site. In the 16th century the house was replaced by a medieval castle with a splendid Renaissance edifice, and the Petit Château was built next to it. In 1662 Le Nôtre remodelled the gardens and park. One of Louis Philippe's sons, the Duc d'Aumale, rebuilt the Grand Château, damaged during the Revolution. On his death in 1897, he left the whole estate to the nation, including his magnificent art collections, which form the basis of the Condé museum.

The museum

In the Petit Château are the former private apartments. The library contains the precious 15th-century illuminated manuscript of *Les Très Riches Heures du Duc de Berry*. In the chapel there is an altar carved by Jean Goujon and 16th-century stained glass, and in the Grand Château, there are paintings by Poussin, Corot, Raphaël, Watteau, Ingres and Botticelli, a unique collection of portraits by Clouet, father and son, and the famous *Grand Condé* diamond stolen in 1926 but found later in an apple where it had been hidden by the thieves.

The park

Most of Le Nôtre's masterpiece of landscape gardening remains: the grand canal and its waterfall, and the shorter canal lined with formal gardens leading to the raised terrace. The *hameau* (hamlet), added in the 18th century, is similar to the more famous one in Versailles. The Jardin Anglais (English garden) was designed in 1820.

The Grandes Ecuries

The vast stable was designed in the 18th century to house 250 horses, 500 dogs and 100 attendants. It is now a museum. The *Prix du Jockey-Club-Lancia* and the *Prix de Diane-Hermès* are run every year in June on the beautiful racecourse in front of the stables.
35km north of Paris. Open: 10.30am–5.30pm. Closed: Tuesday. Admission charge.

CHARTRES

Chartres is the main town of the vast plain of la Beauce, 85km southwest of Paris. In the centre of the old town, on the left bank of the River Eure, stands one of the most beautiful cathedrals in France. Rebuilt in the space of 25 years after a fire destroyed part of the Romanesque edifice in 1194, spared by wars and revolutions, the cathedral is a unique example of French early-Gothic style showing remarkable architectural unity. Pilgrims have been flocking to Chartres since medieval times and, in 1935, students started their own pilgrimage, which takes place every year at the end of April.

The façade

The originality of the façade stems from the contrast between the sombre outline of the Clocher Vieux on the right, in pure Romanesque style, and the rich decoration of the slightly taller spire of the Clocher Neuf, added in 1506. The Portail Royal, famous for its series of tall, column-like figures, and the three windows above it are 12th-century, the rest being 13th-century. The portals of the north and south transepts, dating from the 13th century, are equally remarkable.

The interior

The proportions are vast, with an overall length of 130m and a height of 37m. The Gothic nave, the widest in France, appears relatively short in comparison with the transept and chancel. In the faint light, the deep rich colours of the stained glass windows, dating from the 12th and 13th centuries, immediately capture the attention. The elaborate choir-screen with its 41 groups of sculptures, depicting the life of Christ and the Virgin Mary, was designed in 1514 by Jehan de Beauce. The crypt is the largest in France and the oldest part of the cathedral, and there are traces of a Gallo-Roman wall and a 33m-deep well.

Admission charge to the crypt and gallery of the Clocher Neuf.

The old town between the cathedral and the river has been renovated and offers a pleasant journey back in time, especially along the rue des Ecuyers and adjacent streets.

Château de Chantilly, full of treasures

COURANCES

The Château de Courances is situated 55km south of Paris in wooded country. It is near the small town of Milly-La-Forêt, famous for its beautiful 15th-century covered market.

The original Renaissance castle was remodelled in the early 17th century into a fine example of Louis XIII style. The intricate design of the brick panels, accentuated by stone borders, is offset by the absence of decoration, while the steep slate roofs add an interesting contrast of colours. The outline of the strictly symmetrical edifice is enhanced by the softness of the green setting, reflected in the water of the moat and artificial lakes. A copy of the famous staircase at Fontainebleau was added in the 19th century. The castle is still inhabited and only open at weekends.

The gardens were planned by Le Nôtre, who gave a romantic aspect to his masterly design through the use of reflection in the water of several canals supplied by the near-by River Ecole. *Guided visits on weekend afternoons 2pm–6.30pm, from April to October. Tel: 45 50 34 24. Admission charge. This visit can be combined with that of the Château de Fontainebleau, 17km to the east.*

DAMPIERRE

About 36km southwest of Paris, Dampierre-en-Yvelines is a small community situated at the heart of the parc naturel régional de la Haute Vallée de Chevreuse, a protected rural area. The castle stands out against the dark wooded setting of the vast park laid out by Le Nôtre.

The 16th-century castle, rebuilt in the late 17th century for Colbert's son-in-law, has been the property of the Luynes family ever since; it was restored during the first half of the 19th century. The elegant brick and stone façade, is flanked by two arcaded buildings on either side.

The ground-floor reception rooms have Louis XIV and Louis XV wood panelling. On the first floor are the royal apartments, splendidly decorated to honour the monarchs who stayed at Dampierre on various occasions: Louis XIV, Louis XV and Louis XVI. At the top of the monumental staircase, the large reception room decorated with murals by Ingres is most remarkable. A colourful floral garden occupies part of the park.

Handsomely proportioned Dampierre castle

Château de Dampierre, tel: 30 52 53 24.
Open: every afternoon from April to mid-
October. Admission charge.

ECOUEN

Ecouen is a peaceful community in the
green belt surrounding Paris. It is barely
20km north of the city and is famous for
its Renaissance castle, which houses the
Musée National de la Renaissance.

The castle was built in the early 16th
century for Anne de Montmorency. Like
Chantilly, Ecouen became the property
of the Condé family from whom it was
confiscated during the 1789 Revolution.
It was later used by Napoleon as a
school for the daughters of members of
the Légion d'Honneur. The façade is
adorned with columns and surmounted
by dormer windows with carved
pediments. It has recently been turned
into a museum of Renaissance art to
relieve the overcrowded Musée de Cluny
(see page 90).

Furniture, wood panels, tapestries,
ceramics – 8,000 exhibits in all are displayed in 34 rooms, which have retained
their original decoration whenever
possible, in particular their painted
mantelpieces. On the ground floor there
is a superb collection of arms; on the
first floor, the private apartments of
Montmorency and his wife have some
interesting furniture, while a fine 16th-
century tapestry, 75m long, takes up the
whole of one wing. On the second floor,
there are numerous 16th- and 17th-
century ceramic compositions, some
stained glass with religious motifs, some
painted wood panels, enamels, and so on.
Château d'Ecouen, tel: 39 90 04 04. Open:
9.45am–12.30pm and 2pm–5.15pm.
Closed on Tuesday. Admission charge.
This visit can be combined with an
excursion to the Château de Chantilly.

Gardens at Claude Monet's house, Giverny

GIVERNY

This village, situated near the town of
Vernon, 80km west of Paris, has strong
links with Impressionism through one of
the main exponents of the movement,
the painter Claude Monet, who lived
there from 1883 to his death in 1926.
His house has been turned into a
museum containing mementoes of the
artist and the friends and colleagues who
were his guests. The garden, which he
designed himself, inspired many of his
paintings including the huge *nymphéas*
exhibited in the Musée de l'Orangerie
(see page 94).
Maison de Claude Monet – open April to
October, daily except Monday.
Admission charge.

FONTAINEBLEAU

Set at the heart of a splendid forest, this peaceful residential town lives in the shadow of its beautiful palace. A spring in the middle of the forest determined the choice of Fontainebleau as the site of a royal castle as far back as the 12th century. François I transformed the austere medieval castle into a magnificent Renaissance residence, sparing no expense in decorating the new buildings which form the central part of the palace, and Henri IV extended the palace.

Louis XIV, Louis XV and Louis XVI contributed further to the decoration of the apartments. Spared by the Revolution, the palace continued to be used by kings and emperors until the end of the 19th century, when it was turned into a museum.

Double horseshoe staircase, Fontainebleau

The exterior

The buildings surround four courtyards. Access to the palace is through the main courtyard, or Cour du Cheval Blanc. At the end of the courtyard is the famous 'horseshoe' staircase, from which Napoleon made a very emotional farewell to his imperial guard before his departure to Elba in 1814. Beyond is the Cour de la Fontaine, backed by the Galerie François I. The Cour de la Fontaine overlooks the Etang des Carpes, a small carp pond with a charming pavilion in its centre. Le Nôtre's formal garden is on one side of the pond and the Jardin Anglais (English-style garden) is on the other side. In the centre of the latter is the Fontaine Bliaud. The oldest part of the palace surrounds the Cour Ovale. A monumental entrance gives access to the Cour des Offices which is lined with outbuildings dating from 1609.

The interior

The Grands Appartements (state apartments) on the first floor start with the Galerie François I, with its original Renaissance decoration of stuccos and frescos. The Escalier du Roi leads to the magnificent Salle de Bal (ballroom); the ceiling and chimney-piece are particularly remarkable. On the other side of the Cour Ovale are the Appartements Royaux, the monarchs' private and official apartments, which include the Salon du Donjon, the only remaining part of the medieval castle, and the Salle du Trône, formerly the king's bedroom. In the emperor's official apartments is the famous Salon Rouge, where he abdicated in 1814.

The Petits Appartements on the ground floor were the private apartments of Napoleon and Joséphine, and contain

The Tapestry Salon at Fontainebleau

some splendid Empire furniture.
60km southeast of Paris; entrance place du
Général de Gaulle. Tel: 64 22 27 40.
Open: 9.30am–12.30pm and 2pm–5pm.
Closed on Tuesday. Admission charge.

ROYAUMONT

The Cistercian abbey of Royaumont,
founded by Saint-Louis in 1228 and
richly endowed by his successors,
remained very powerful until the Revolution. The church was then demolished
and the extensive abbey buildings turned
into a cotton mill. Royaumont, now
owned by a foundation, is the scene of
regular cultural activities.

Very little remains of the church.
Next to it, the cloister, which encloses a
garden, is the largest of any Cistercian
abbey in France. The long refectory,
where Saint-Louis served the monks

himself during his visits to the abbey, is a
masterpiece of early Gothic architecture.
In the kitchens, the impressive vaulted
ceiling rests on massive columns with
fine carved capitals.
30km north of Paris. Tel: 30 35 40 18.
Tours: mid-March to October, daily except
Tuesday. Admission charge. This excursion
can be combined with a trip to Chantilly.

ST-GERMAIN-EN-LAYE

This important residential town, 18km
west of Paris, has a history going back to
the building of the first castle in the 12th
century. The Renaissance castle erected
in 1539 by Pierre Chambiges on the
same site was later extended by Jules
Hardouin-Mansart and the park and
gardens designed by Le Nôtre, including
a magnificent Grande Terrasse, 2.4km
long.

In 1855, Napoleon III restored the
castle to its original state and set up the
Musée des Antiquités Nationales. The
museum's archaeological collections
cover France's past from the Palaeolithic
period to the Dark Ages, and include a
reconstruction of the famous Salle des
Taureaux at Lascaux.
Place du Château. Tel: 34 51 53 65. Open:
9am–5.15pm. Closed on Tuesday.
Admission charge, free on Wednesday. RER
St-Germain-en-Laye.

Castle museum of St-Germain-en-Laye

Theme Parks

*T*his popular form of family entertainment is represented in the Paris region by Euro Disney, the latest arrival on the scene, some 32km east of the capital, France Miniature 25km west, and the Parc Astérix 25km north.

Euro Disney – where shall we go now?

EURO DISNEY

The theme park which is at the heart of Euro Disney is in fact only part of a vast holiday resort covering nearly 2,000 hectares. Also here are six hotels, campsites, restaurants, shops, a golf course, tennis courts and plenty of night entertainment.

Euro Disney is an extraordinary mixture of fantasy (Walt Disney's fairy-tale characters brought to life, and flying machines that take you into the future)

and adventure (in the company of pirates, cowboys and Indians). Embark on an astonishing voyage with the pioneers of yesterday and those of tomorrow, through a magical kingdom where the only frontiers are those of your own imagination. The key word is enjoyment.

Marne-la-Vallée. Tel: 64 74 30 00. Open: all year, daily 9am–10pm with seasonal variations. Admission charge: one, two or three-day 'passports' available. RER Chessy (end of the line).

FRANCE MINIATURE

As its title implies, this theme park will take you on a lightning journey across France, to see the country as Gulliver saw the land of Lilliput, travelling from one region to the next in a few minutes. Two thousand models reduced 30 times, including 140 monuments, 20 typical villages, landscapes and scenes of daily life, are spread over a vast relief map of France that covers 5 hectares.

There are shops selling craft and other products from the regions of France, exhibitions, stands where you can sample regional cuisine, a picnic area and two restaurants.

25 route du Mesnil, Elancourt. Tel: 30 51 51 51. Open: April to 15 November, 10am–7pm, Friday and Saturday till 11pm, 10am–8pm July and August. Admission charge. RER St-Quentin-en-Yvelines, then shuttle service to the theme park.

PARC ASTÉRIX

The setting is France under Roman occupation 2,000 years ago, seen through the eyes of the characters created by Albert Uderzo for his series of *Astérix* comic strips, in which the intelligent and cunning Gauls constantly outwit the dumb Romans.

Astérix, the hero, is the brain behind the action and Obelix, his fat devoted friend, lends him his muscle power, with Getafix the druid and many others. But there is more. Parc Astérix is an adventure park with many outdoor activities for the whole family; shops in Via Antiqua and rue de Paris, a medieval square with its crowd of jugglers and acrobats, and two restaurants.

60128 Plailly. Tel: 44 62 31 31. Open: April to October 10am–6pm, weekend 7pm. Admission charge. RER Roissy, then shuttle service to the park.

VAUX-LE-VICOMTE

Situated 50km southeast of Paris, the Château de Vaux-le-Vicomte is a masterpiece of 17th-century French architecture. Fouquet, Louis XIV's finance minister, had gathered a colossal fortune and decided to build a castle that would be a symbol of his success. He commissioned the best artists of his time, no expense was spared. The castle was completed in just five years, and Fouquet invited Louis XIV to a splendid reception that greatly surpassed those given at court. The king was so annoyed that he had Fouquet – who had already fallen from favour – arrested a few days later. After a lengthy trial the ambitious minister was condemned to life imprisonment. The castle changed hands several times during the next 200 years until it was bought by a rich industrialist, whose family have since restored both house and gardens.

The main building stands on a raised terrace surrounded by a moat. On the ground floor, six reception rooms on either side of the oval Grand Salon (drawing-room) overlook the magnificent gardens. The frescos on the ceilings, depicting mythological scenes, are by Le Brun.

A staircase in the entrance hall gives access to the first floor private apartments. From the terrace, the view sweeps across the gardens, which extend a long way on different levels and are adorned with ornamental ponds, cascades and a Grand Canal. In the stables there is a museum of horse-drawn carriages.

Vaux-le-Vicomte, 77950 Maincy, near Melun. Tel: 60 66 97 09. Open: April to October 10am–6pm, November to March 11am–5pm. Admission charge. Visit by candlelight every Saturday from May to September, 8.30pm–11pm; cafeteria.

Escape to amusement at Parc Astérix

Versailles

*F*or most people, Versailles is the supreme example of an aspect of French culture that blends elegance and refinement with a search for perfection, and that is sometimes coupled with excessive formality and bold confidence.

A most ambitious project

In 1661, Louis XIV, the Sun King, decided to build a castle that would outshine Vaux-le-Vicomte (see page 129) on the site of the modest brick and stone château built by Philibert Le Roy for his father in 1631. For nearly 50 years the greatest artists worked at Versailles: the architect, Le Vau succeeded by Hardouin-Mansart; Le Brun, who supervised the interior decoration; and Le Nôtre, who surpassed himself in the design of the magnificent gardens. The King and his court moved in during 1682 – a total of 3,000 people, attending sumptuous receptions! Versailles was also the political centre of France from 1682 to 1789.

During the Revolution, the furniture was sold and the château gradually fell into disrepair until, in 1837, Louis-Philippe had it converted into a museum of French history.

After World War I, a complete restoration of the castle was undertaken with the financial help of J D Rockfeller, and Versailles has slowly regained its 18th-century elegance.

The château

The approach to the château, one of the most visited monuments in France, is very impressive with its succession of three open courtyards, the Court of Ministers, the Royal Court and the Court of Marble, and Louis XIV's statue in the centre.

On the garden side, the 680m long façade has a projecting central section. An elegant balustrade emphasises the roof line, and groups of columns at regular intervals act as focal points.

Grands Appartements

On the way to the State Apartments, it is possible to have a look at the chapel, designed by Hardouin-Mansart but only completed after his death in 1710. The State Apartments include a suite of reception rooms, decorated with marble and paintings depicting mythological scenes; they were used for the entertainment of the court during the winter season.

The large windows of the 75m long Galerie des Glaces (Hall of Mirrors), the most famous room in the palace, overlooking the gardens, let in the setting sun which reflects on the huge mirrors (not the original glass) covering the walls. Next come the Queen's Apartments, in particular the Queen's bedroom where Louis XV and many royal children were born – in public.

The King's Apartments are in Louis XIII's castle. The king's bedroom, remodelled by Louis XIV, was used by his successors until 1789. Next door is the Chambre du Conseil (Council Chamber), where political decisions were traditionally taken.

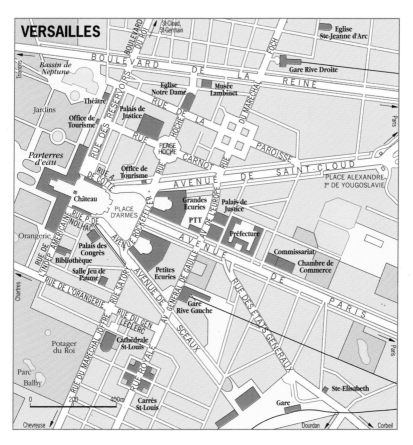

VERSAILLES

St-Cloud, St-Germain

Eglise Ste-Jeanne d'Arc

Trianons

Bassin de Neptune

BOULEVARD DU ROI

BOULEVARD DE LA REINE

Gare Rive Droite

Paris

FOCH

Jardins

Théâtre

Eglise Notre Dame

Musée Lambinet

Office de Tourisme

Palais de Justice

RUE DES RÉSERVOIRS

RUE DE LA PAROISSE

Parterres d'eau

RUE DE COLTE

Office de Tourisme

PLACE HOCHE

RUE HOCHE

CARNOT

AVENUE DE SAINT-CLOUD

PLACE ALEXANDRE-Iᵉʳ DE YOUGOSLAVIE

Château

PLACE D'ARMES

Grandes Ecuries

Palais de Justice

RUE P-DE NOLHAC

AVENUE ROCKEFELLER

PTT

AVENUE DE L'EUROPE

Préfecture

Orangerie

RUE DE L'INDÉPENDANCE AMÉRICAINE

Palais des Congrès

Bibliothèque

Salle Jeu de Paume

Petites Ecuries

AVENUE DE SATORY

AVENUE DE GÉNÉRAL DE GAULLE

Commissariat

Chambre de Commerce

AVENUE DE PARIS

Paris

Chartres

RUE DE L'ORANGERIE

Gare Rive Gauche

RUE DES ÉTATS-GÉNÉRAUX

RUE DU GEN LECLERC

RUE DU MARÉCHAL JOFFRE

Potager du Roi

Cathédrale St-Louis

RUE ROYALE

AVENUE DE SCEAUX

Parc Balby

0   200   400m

Carrés St-Louis

Ste-Elisabeth

Gare

Chevreuse

Dourdan

Corbeil

Château de Versailles, place d'Armes. Tel: 30 84 74 00. RER Versailles-Rive gauche. Open: daily except Monday. Admission charge; parking free. Château: 9.45am–5.30pm;

Park: 7am–dusk. Visits – without guide: Chapelle, Grands Appartements; entrance A on the right. With guide: Appartement du Roi, last visit starts at 4pm.

Tuesday to Friday only: Appartements du Dauphin, de la Dauphine et de Mesdames at 2pm. Events: every Sunday from May to October the numerous fountains are turned on at 3.30pm.

Combined fountains and fireworks displays some Saturday nights in summer. For information, contact Tourist Office 7 rue des Réservoirs. Tel: 39 50 36 22.

Versailles

Cabinets Intérieurs du Roi

The King's private apartments, designed by Gabriel for Louis XV, include the bedroom where the King died in 1774, the games room, the study with its original desk, the music room, which Louis XV furnished for his favourite daughter, Madame Adélaïde, and where the young Wolfgang Mozart is supposed to have played in 1763, and the beautiful library.

The Cabinets Intérieurs de la Reine were private apartments originally designed for Louix XV's queen, and were later refurbished for Marie-Antoinette.

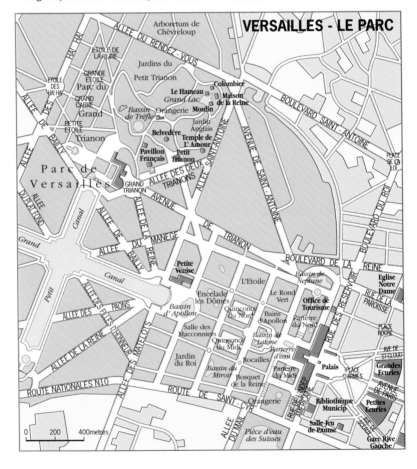

VERSAILLES - LE PARC

Opéra Royal

Built by Gabriel, the opera house was inaugurated in 1770 for the wedding of Marie-Antoinette to the future Louis XVI. It could seat 700 spectators, and could also be used as a grand reception room or a ballroom.

On the ground floor are the recently renovated appartements du Dauphin et de la Dauphine (the heirs to the throne) and those of Louis XV's daughters.

The gardens

From the raised terrace in front of the château, the Grand Canal offers a magnificent vista which extends to the woods in the distance. The design of the gardens by Le Nôtre, between 1661 and 1668, is a masterpiece of geometry: the canal is the focal point of a harmonious composition on different levels, comprising ornamental ponds adorned with fountains, flower beds, bowers and over 200 sculptures.

The Trianons

The Trianons are lesser palaces. The Grand Trianon, faced with pink marble, was built by Hardouin-Mansart for Louis XIV, who wished to give private receptions for Madame de Maintenon.

The Petit Trianon was commissioned by Louis XV and given by Louis XVI to Marie-Antoinette who used it to be alone with her children. She had the garden completely remodelled and the charming _hameau_ (hamlet) built near by.

Cabinets Intérieurs de la Reine – guided tours Tuesday to Friday only at 3.30pm. Opéra Royal – last guided visit starts 4pm. Grand Trianon – open: 9.45am–noon and 2pm–5pm. Petit Trianon – open: 2pm–5pm. Entrance A on the right.

Waterways and fountains in the gardens at Versailles

Getting away from it all

A large city can become oppressive after a while, and you may suddenly feel the need to get away from the crowds and the incessant noise, particularly with the arrival of warm, sunny weather in late spring or summer. Paris and the Ile-de-France offer plenty of opportunities for a change of pace and scenery, in parks and floral gardens, in forests teeming with wildlife and along quiet rivers.

IN OR NEAR PARIS

Paris has a fair number of parks and gardens and two areas of woodland that were once part of royal hunting forests, the Bois de Boulogne on the west side and the Bois de Vincennes on the east side.

The Bois: Paris' peace of the countryside

BOIS DE BOULOGNE

This favourite haunt of nature-loving Parisians, covering about 850 hectares, is crowded at weekends, but offers peace and quiet to those who wander off the beaten track along its shady alleys (take care after dusk). Many activities suitable for the whole family are available: boating on the lakes, cycling along specially designed lanes, horse-riding and fishing. The Jardin d'Acclimatation, on the northern edge of the 'Bois', is a comprehensive amusement park for children (see page 159); near by is the Musée des Arts et Traditions Populaires (see page 111) and there are clearly marked picnic areas.

This former royal hunting forest used to abound with deer, bear and wild boar until Louis XV opened it to the public and it became fashionable. Given to the city of Paris in 1852 by Napoleon III, it was remodelled into an English-style park by Baron Haussmann, who created lakes, ponds and the Longchamp racecourse. The Auteuil racecourse was built after the Franco-Prussian War in 1870 and at the turn of the century fashionable horse-drawn carriages could be seen driving along the wide avenues that nowadays carry fast traffic bound for the *banlieue* (suburbs) just across the Seine.

In the northwest corner of the 'Bois' is the Parc de Bagatelle, a beautiful garden well known for its spring display of tulips and irises, and for its roses and water-lilies in summer. The nearby Jardins de Bagatelle is an expensive restaurant in a lovely setting.

The Pré Catelan, in the centre of the Bois de Boulogne, is another attractive park with a magnificent 200-year-old copper beech; next to it, the Jardin Shakespeare, planted with flowers and trees mentioned in Shakespeare's plays, has a charming open-air theatre.

Access: north side, métro Les Sablons; Bagatelle, métro Pont-de-Neuilly then no 43 bus to place de Bagatelle; east side, RER avenue-Henri-Martin, bicycle rental available at the lakes, horse-riding at the Centre Hippique, route de la Muette à Neuilly, tel: 40 67 95 52; south side, métro Porte-d'Auteuil; for information about fishing, tel: 45 25 58 05.

RACING

There are two racecourses on the south side of the Bois de Boulogne. Auteuil specialises in steeple chasing and is famous for its difficult jumps, which include an 8m water-jump. Flat racing takes place at Longchamp. Prestigious races such as the *Prix du Président de la République* on Palm Sunday or the *Grand Prix de l'Arc de Triomphe* on the first Sunday in October draw fashionable crowds, who come more to be seen than to watch the racing. The Vincennes racecourse, situated on the other side of town, is popular for trotting events.

BOIS DE VINCENNES

See page 121.

JARDIN ALBERT-KAHN

Situated just south of the Bois de Boulogne, this succession of gardens, created by the banker Albert Khan, illustrates landscapes from different regions of the world: the forest of the Vosges region, a Japanese garden, an English garden and a picturesque rock setting. The display of hundreds of flowers is at its best in late spring.

1 rue des Abondances, 92100 Boulogne. Open: 11am–6pm. Admission charge.

Orangerie, parc de Bagatelle, the Bois

Métro Pont-de-St-Cloud then no 72, 52 or 175 bus.

JARDIN FLEURISTE DE LA VILLE DE PARIS

Plants used for decorating public buildings and for official occasions are grown in the greenhouses surrounding this municipal garden, while the huge tropical house contains palm trees, banana trees and a host of tropical plants. Rare species are housed in a number of hothouses on the south side of the garden.

3 avenue de la Porte d'Auteuil, 75016. Open: 10am–5pm. Admission charge. Métro Porte d'Auteuil.

The Role of the River

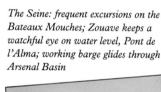

The Seine: frequent excursions on the Bateaux Mouches; Zouave keeps a watchful eye on water level, Pont de l'Alma; working barge glides through Arsenal Basin

The Seine played a vital role in the birth and development of the city of Paris. The first settlers to occupy the area were fishermen and for hundreds of years the river provided food, water and protection to the people who lived on the Ile-de-la-Cité. When commerce became essential to the survival of the rapidly developing city, the Seine was the obvious means of communications and proved quite lucrative for those who levied substantial tolls.

Because the economy of Paris depended on the river, it was natural that those who sought to rule the city should also seek to control its main port which in medieval times was La Grève (now the place de l'Hôtel de Ville). In the 13th century, the guild of merchants obtained from the king the right to levy taxes from ships bringing in essential goods such as salt, wine and wood; the harbour developed rapidly and today Paris is the main river port and the fourth most important harbour in France.

The Seine has contributed so much to their prosperity, that Parisians really love their river. They have built their most prestigious monuments along its banks; they have adorned it with beautiful bridges; and lined its embankment with trees to provide shade so that they could stroll there after a day's work or sit on one of the benches and relax in the cool of the evening.

The river's sometimes erratic behaviour can now be controlled, but memorable floods have been recorded in the past, and when the river happens to rise above its normal level, people still flock eagerly to the Pont de l'Alma to see how much of the famous *Zouave* is under water.

JARDIN DES PLANTES

Founded in 1626, the botanical gardens were greatly extended by the famous 18th-century naturalist, Buffon, and the menagerie was created during the Revolution. The Musée d'Histoire Naturelle (Museum of Natural History) houses departments of botany, mineralogy, palaeontology and entomology. The gardens include the Jardin Alpin with 2,000 species of plants from mountainous regions from the Alps to the Himalayas, the Jardin d'Hiver, housing heavy-scented tropical plants and flowers, a number of hothouses, a maze and a herb garden devoted to medicinal plants.

Entrance rue Cuvier, rue Buffon, and place Valhubert, 75005. Tel: 43 36 54 26. Gardens open: 8am–8pm in summer; menagerie 9am–6pm; museum and maze 10am–5pm. Admission charge. Métro Gare d'Austerlitz or Jussieu.

Delightfully landscaped Parc Monceau includes a water feature

PARC DES BUTTES-CHAUMONT

Situated in the 19th *arrondissement,* east of the centre, this park was landscaped by Haussmann on hilly wasteland. From the small temple, romantically set on the island in the middle of the lake, the view extends to the Butte Montmartre.
Métro Buttes-Chaumont or Botzaris.

PARC GEORGES BRASSENS

Two bronze bulls at the main entrance are a reminder that the park was created on the site of the former Vaugirard slaughterhouses. A small garden filled with scented plants was specially designed for blind people, and the vineyard is the scene of festivities during the grape harvest in October.
Rue des Morillons, 75015. Métro Convention.

PARC MONCEAU

Situated in a fashionable residential area, close to the Arc de Triomphe, the Parc Monceau was landscaped as an English garden, with rocks and an oddly shaped lake and adorned with mock ruins, pyramids and statues following the neoclassical style fashionable in the 18th century.

Boulevard de Courcelles. Métro Monceau.

PARC MONTSOURIS

Another of Haussmann's creations, this hilly park facing the Cité Universitaire (the student halls of residence) includes a large lake, waterfalls, a meteorological observatory and a reproduction of the Bardo, the Bey of Tunis's palace.

Boulevard Jourdan. RER Cité-Universitaire.

PARC DE ST-CLOUD

Situated in one of the elegant western suburbs overlooking the Seine, this park was designed by Le Nôtre. The castle, where Napoleon stayed many times, was destroyed by fire in 1870. The Grand Cascade, with its statues featuring the Seine and the Marne rivers, is particularly remarkable; so is the view across Paris from the terrace. The woods in the upper part of the park offer lovely cool walks in summer.

On the N186, 11km west of Paris.

OUT OF TOWN

The green belt round Paris includes several woodland areas, the largest being the Fôret de Rambouillet and the Fôret de Fontainebleau. Many rivers wind their way towards the Seine along picturesque valleys like the Vallée de Chevreuse with its quiet, twisting roads. And, of course, the ideal means to achieve complete relaxation is to join a leisurely cruise along the Seine for a few hours, or even a whole day.

FÔRET DE FONTAINEBLEAU

This vast forest surrounding the castle and town of Fontainebleau over an area of 25,000 hectares offers a landscape of wooded hills and valleys, of moors covered with heather and gorse, and of large rocks piled high in places. Pines, oaks and beeches make up the majority of the forest. There are opportunities for rock-climbing and the area has become popular with amateurs and professionals.

Various itineraries are suggested in the _Guide des sentiers de promenades dans le Massif forestier de Fontainebleau,_ available from the tourist office in Fontainebleau. Most tours start from the town. To the west are the Gorges de Franchard, a narrow glen scattered with impressive overhanging rocks. To the south, le Long Rocher is a rock-strewn plateau that affords lovely views over the forest.

60km southeast of Paris.

Spend the day in Fontainebleau forest

WILDLIFE

You do not have to be an expert to appreciate the subtle blend of colours and the fresh scent of woodland flowers in springtime in the Fôret de Fontainebleau. Hyacinths, daffodils and laburnum herald the return of the warm weather, followed by hawthorn blossoms and fragile lilies-of-the-valley. Later on, dense bushes of gorse light up the green undergrowth, eclipsing the more discreet heather, campanulas and wild carnations. Summer offers the pleasure of looking for wild strawberries and raspberries, while autumn brings hazelnuts and chestnuts. These traditional hunting grounds still abound with roe deer and boar as well as the more common foxes, hares and squirrels. There is also a great variety of birdlife, including the famous Fontainebleau woodpeckers.

FÔRET DE RAMBOUILLET

Although less spectacular than Fontainebleau, this forest, covering 20,000 hectares, offers pleasant walks and cycle tours through ancient villages, along narrow rivers and beside picturesque lakes. Oaks and pines are predominant, and red deer and wild boar are plentiful, if not always easy to detect.

In the isolated northern part of the forest, fishermen seek peace and quiet on the shores of the Etang Neuf, near the solitary 16th-century castle of La Mormaire and the almost deserted village of Gambaiseuil. Further south, from the Rochers d'Angennes, a rock formation on high ground, there is a good view of the Etang d'Angennes, overgrown with reeds, and the secluded valley of the Guesle River.

South of Rambouillet, the Parc Animalier des Yveslines (parking and entrance on the D27) is a nature reserve covering 250 hectares where roe deer, red deer, fallow deer and boars can be seen roaming peacefully.

50km southwest of Paris. Parc Animalier – tel: 34 84 51 21. Open: Wednesday and Saturday afternoons, all day Sunday, every afternoon except Tuesday in July and August. Closed: May and June. Admission charge.

L'HAŸ-LES-ROSES

Situated in the densely populated southern suburbs, halfway between Paris and Orly Airport, the rose garden of L'Haÿ-les-Roses was created 100 years ago; thousands of roses, wild ones as well as hybrids, offer a magnificent display of colours in a charming setting framed with climbers. There is also a Musée de la Rose, devoted to works of art connected with this aristocratic flower: prints, embroidery, ceramics and small *objets d'art*.

8km south of Paris.

PARC DE SCEAUX

This might be the right place to start exploring the Paris region, since the Château de Sceaux houses the Musée de l'Ile-de-France, which provides a wealth of information about the area as a whole, its landscapes, cultural heritage and less well-known aspects.

The gardens were designed by Le Nôtre and Louis XIV was invited to a splendid reception to mark the inauguration of the castle, built in 1670. During the revolution, the estate was bought for the use of the land and the castle was demolished. The state acquired the property in 1923, undertook its restoration and opened the Musée de l'Ile-de-France.

Once more, water is the focal point of the beautiful gardens by Le Nôtre: on the south side, a wide avenue leads to the Grandes Cascades, a succession of waterfalls supplying an octagonal lake surrounded by plane trees reflected in the still water; the grand canal is also lined with trees, which create contrasts of sunlight and shade and temper the formal aspect of French-style gardens.

The Petit Château and the Pavillon de L'Aurore date from the 17th century. In the latter there is an audiovisual presentation of the estate.

10km southwest of Paris. Museum – tel: 46 61 06 71. Open 10am–noon and 2pm–6pm. Closed: Monday and Friday morning, all day Tuesday. Admission charge. RER Parc de Sceaux.

ST-VRAIN

This safari park covers 130 hectares of woodland with ponds and canals supplied by the nearby River Juine. One of the attractions of the park is the *safari-bateau,* which enables visitors to get close to the birds, chimpanzees and gibbons living on the islands. It is also possible to tour the park aboard a monorail, from which one gets a good overall view. In one section of the park, lifesize reproductions of prehistoric animals and men have been set up in a re-created environment.

45km south of Paris. tel: 64 56 10 80. Open: April to October. Admission charge.

VALLÉE DE CHEVREUSE

The upper valley of the River Yvette is known as the Vallée de Chevreuse, after the small town dominated by the ruins of its castle. In 1984, a regional park was created to preserve this area of natural beauty, consisting of woodland, lush meadows and cultivated land. The D58, which follows the river westwards, leads to the Château de Dampierre (see page 124). To the north are the ruins of the Cistercian abbey of Port-Royal-des-Champs, famous in the 17th century for its criticism of the Jesuits. The southern road (D24) leads to Les Vaux de Cernay, where a picturesque stream makes its way through woods and rocks.

The town of Chevreuse is situated 30km southwest of Paris.

Walk or cycle in Fôret de Rambouillet

Shopping

*P*art of the fun of staying in Paris is to go on a shopping spree. Deciding where to go, however, can be quite bewildering in any large city and particularly in Paris, where attractive shop windows are to be found round every street corner.

If you have set ideas from the start and know exactly what you want, the section 'Where to find what you are looking for' at the end of this chapter will be of help. If, however, you just want to window shop, there are many possibilities waiting to be discovered all over town, from the luxury and fashion boutiques of the 8th and 9th *arrondissements* to the flea-market on the northern fringe of the city.

Village-style shopping, rue Mouffetard

Suggestions

Before you embark on a shopping tour of Paris there are a few facts you should be aware of.

It is dangerous to carry large amounts of cash as pickpockets are on the look out in crowded places. The safest and now the most widely used method of payment in boutiques, department stores and shopping centres is by credit card;

but bear in mind that a minimum purchase of 100 francs is required.

Be prepared to pay cash, however, at market stalls and food kiosks.

Tax-free shopping is now common practice; look out for the symbol on shop windows. If you are a resident of a country outside the EC, you need to spend a minimum of 2,000 francs to qualify for a tax refund; if you reside within the EC, you need to spend at least 4,200 francs on one item. You are then given a special bill in two parts; the shopkeeper will tell you where to send one of the copies for a VAT refund, once it has been stamped by customs.

Although shops remain open quite late in the evening (see the **Practical Guide**), individual shops are often closed on Monday morning, sometimes all day Monday, and if you are planning a long weekend in Paris, it is preferable to opt for Friday rather than Monday.

Department stores

All the large department stores except one are situated on the right bank. Moreover, Parisians often refer to the St-Lazare-Opéra district as the *quartier des grands magasins,* as the most prestigious of them are lined up along the boulevard Haussmann.

The Galeries Lafayette, 40 boulevard Haussmann, 75009, tel: 42 82 34 56, métro Chaussée d'Antin and the Printemps, 64 boulevard Haussmann, 75009, tel: 42 82 50 00, métro Havre-Caumartin, both established in the late 19th century, tend to lay the emphasis more and more on elegance and fashion trends in clothes and accessories as well as household goods. Their extensive ready-to-wear departments have attracted all the main designers, who have their own stands within the department. The Printemps has devoted a separate building to men's wear (Brummell). Cosmetics and perfume are lavishly displayed on the ground floor and both stores have comprehensive book and record departments as well as restaurants which are particularly crowded on Saturdays.

On the other side of the busy boulevard Haussmann, Marks and Spencer has acquired a faithful clientele through its up-market prepared-food department.

Two other department stores situated between the Louvre and the Hôtel de Ville, along the rue de Rivoli, are less fashion conscious and mainly sought after for their household goods. The Bazar de l'Hôtel de Ville, known as the BHV, 52 rue de Rivoli, 75004, tel: 42 74 90 00, métro Hôtel de Ville, has an incredibly well-stocked DIY department in the basement. Near by, the Samaritaine, 19 rue de la Monnaie, 75001, tel: 40 41 20 20, métro Pont-Neuf, which attracts a similar clientele, was recently renovated and you can now enjoy a cup of tea on the roof terrace while admiring the splendid view over Paris.

Galeries Lafayette: shop till you drop

The Bon Marché, 38 rue de Sèvres, 75007, tel: 42 60 33 45, métro Sèvres-Babylone, the only department store on the Left Bank, is rightly famous for its fine food section, l'Epicerie, which is open longer hours than the store itself.

Arcades

Quaint, old-fashioned and full of atmosphere, some of these arcades make a change from traditional shopping (see page 110).

Markets

*M*arkets still represent a significant aspect of Parisian life, the continuation of an old tradition, which has its beginnings back in the Middle Ages.

OPEN-AIR MARKETS

These are the most ancient type of markets, but they have, for some time, been in fierce competition with the large supermarkets to supply Parisian households with fresh food. However, this is one battle the big stores are not about to win, for not only do open-air markets offer their demanding customers good quality and low prices, but they are also the very fibre of a district's social life, a meeting-place where neighbours of different backgrounds exchange opinions.

Some of these markets are organised by the municipality and usually take place on two or three mornings a week, on a square or large open space. Canopied stalls are put up the night before, and early in the morning stall holders park their vans all around, usually creating huge traffic jams. They come straight from the central food market at Rungis, and their prices are very competitive indeed. Two such markets can be found in the Latin Quarter on the place Monge (métro Monge) and the place Maubert (métro Maubert-Mutualité).

Street markets usually run on a slightly different principle. Shops that sell fresh food in a particular street set up stands outside their premises on every day of the week except one, and advertise special offers. Greengrocers attract a large clientele, but cheese stalls are also popular, and chickens are frequently seen roasting outside butchers' shops. These markets are open until early evening to enable working people to get their daily supply of fresh

Always appealing, fresh produce at keen prices in a Montparnasse street market

vegetables on their way home. The rue Mouffetard (métro Censier-Daubenton) and the rue de Buci (métro Mabillon) markets in the Latin Quarter are among the best in Paris; the rue Lepic in Montmartre (métro Blanche) is also very attractive and lively.

Assessing a find in the stamp market

COVERED MARKETS

These are also steeped in tradition as they are the direct descendants of medieval structures known as *halles*, which usually consisted of a solid roof resting on large wooden pillars. With the development of the city, covered markets were implanted in outlying districts and their appearance changed considerably. Today they are housed in proper buildings belonging to the municipality. They have cubicles all round and fixed stalls in the centre where carefully selected shopkeepers offer good service in a friendly atmosphere. In addition to food shops of every kind, some precincts include sub-post offices, cobblers and even opticians. There are 13 covered markets in Paris, all to be found on the Right Bank except one, which is situated in the rue Mabillon in St-Germain-des-Prés (métro Mabillon). Another interesting market is in the rue Lebon,

near the place des Ternes, in the 17th *arrondissement* (métro Ternes).

SPECIALISED MARKETS

The loveliest flower market in Paris is situated on the delightful place Louis-Lépine, a peaceful enclave on the northern side of the Ile-de-la-Cité (métro Cité). It takes place every day from 8am to 7pm, except on Sunday when it is replaced by a bird market.

Another pleasant flower market is held on the place de la Madeleine (métro Madeleine). There is also a small pet market along the quai de la Mégisserie, on the right bank (métro Châtelet or Pont-Neuf).

On the corner of the avenue de Marigny and the avenue Gabriel (métro Champs-Elysées-Clémenceau), an extensive stamp market takes place on Thursdays, Saturdays and Sundays.

Cheap new and second-hand clothes are sold in a covered market every morning except Monday on the Carreau du Temple (métro Temple).

FLEA MARKETS

The most famous flea market in Paris is the Marchés aux Puces of the Porte de Clignancourt, in St-Ouen, which takes place on Saturday, Sunday and Monday between 7am and 7pm. Unfortunately, it has developed into a well-organised trading centre and bargains are very rare these days. The stalls are grouped in eight separate structures according to their speciality.

Other, similar but more genuine markets are held in the open, on Saturday and Sunday along the avenues Georges-Lafenestre and Marc-Sangnier (métro Porte de Vanves), and avenue de la Porte de Montreuil (métro Porte de Montreuil).

Shopping Centres

*I*n places a wide variety of boutiques are gathered under one roof for convenience.

The Forum des Halles, rue Pierre Lescot, métro Les Halles (see page 66), is an underground complex with shops of all sizes selling just about everything you can imagine or want. The galeries des Champs Elysées, on the north side of the famous avenue, between the Rond-Point and the rue de Berri (métro Franklin-Roosevelt), are worth exploring for their elegant boutiques.

The vast shopping complex at La Défense, Les Quatre Temps, has a network of lanes lined with shops on several levels and a huge hypermarket called Auchan.

SPECIALISED STREETS AND AREAS

In the 9th *arrondissement* there are busy shopping streets north of the boulevard Haussmann, with a number of stamp-collectors, high-class confectioners, up-market decorators and fashion boutiques.

Not far from there, in the 8th *arrondissement*, the area round the place de l'Europe is well known for its musical instrument-makers and dealers.

On the place de la Madeleine can be found the finest high-class grocers and delicatessen in Paris: Fauchon and Hédiard.

South of the boulevard Haussmann, the avenue Matignon and rue du Faubourg St-Honoré are famous for their art galleries, while the avenue Montaigne and rue François I are the headquarters of fashion designers; the rue La Boétie counts many antique dealers and the rue de la Paix and place Vendôme are lined with exclusive jewellers. The main glass and china manufacturers have their showrooms along the rue de Paradis, near the gare de l'Est in the 10th *arrondissement*.

On the south bank, the rue du Four, rue Bonaparte and rue de Rennes, near St-Germain-des-Prés in the 6th *arrondissement*, are well-known for their fashion boutiques.

WHERE TO FIND WHAT YOU ARE LOOKING FOR

If you are looking for something specific, the following selection of shops should be of help.

Antiques

Le Louvre des Antiquaires, 2 place du Palais-Royal, tel: 42 97 27 00, métro Palais-Royal; its 250 shops offer plenty of choice.

The shops of the Carré Rive Gauche, formed by the Quai Voltaire, rue des St-Pères, rue de l'Université and rue du Bac, next to the Musée d'Orsay, métro rue du Bac.

The Village Suisse, 78 avenue de Suffren, tel: 43 06 69 90, métro La Motte-Picquet-Grenelle; over 100 dealers sell good quality ornaments and furniture.

The famous auctioneers, Drouot, have salerooms at 9 rue Drouot,

Antiques – worth a glance, browse or buy

tel: 48 00 20 20, métro Richelieu-Drouot, and at 15 avenue Montaigne, tel: 48 00 20 80, métro Alma-Marceau.

Over 50 antique dealers are established in the tiny pedestrian streets of the Village St-Paul in the Marais, métro St-Paul or Pont-Marie.

Books

The largest bookshops in Paris are the book departments of the FNAC stores, in the Forum des Halles and avenue des Ternes (see Hi-fi).

Many traditional bookshops are established in the 6th *arrondissement,* in and around the boulevard St-Germain.

Books in English are available from W H Smith, 248 rue de Rivoli, tel: 42 60 37 97, métro Concorde; Galignani, 224 rue de Rivoli, tel: 42 60 76 07, métro Tuileries; and Brentano's, 37 avenue de l'Opéra, tel: 42 61 52 50, métro Pyramides.

Clothes

Apart from the exclusive fashion designers in the 8th *arrondissement,* there are trendy fashion boutiques in the area round the church of St-Germain-des-Prés, while department stores have a choice of more traditional wear. Bargains can be found in the avenue de Clichy in the 17th *arrondissement.*

Food

See page 164.

Gifts

Replicas from museum exhibits and objects created by famous manufacturers on a theme chosen by the Association Paris-Musées, are sold in the association's four boutiques:

Carnavalet, 23 rue de Sévigné, 75003, métro St-Paul; Forum des Halles, rue Pierre Lescot, métro Les Halles; Le Louvre, métro Palais-Royal; Galliéra, 10 avenue Pierre I de Serbie, 75016, métro Iéna.

See also *les bouquinistes* page 102.

Hi-fi, Compact Discs etc

Three superstores compete to offer the best prices and a vast choice:

FNAC, Forum des Halles, 1 rue Pierre-Lescot, tel: 40 41 40 00, métro Les Halles, RER Châtelet-les-Halles.

FNAC Etoile, 26 avenue des Ternes, tel: 44 09 18 00, métro Ternes.

Virgin Megastore, 52-60 avenue des Champs-Elysées, tel: 40 74 06 48, métro Franklin-Roosevelt.

Jewellery

Rue de la Paix, place Vendôme.

Look for fashion jewellery in the Printemps, the Galeries Lafayette and the Galerie Vivienne (see page 111).

Leather goods

Rue Tronchet, rue St-Lazare and adjacent streets (métro St-Lazare), boulevard St-Michel and near by (métro St-Michel), rue des Archives, Marais (métro Hôtel de Ville).

Luxury goods

Rue Royale (china, crystal), Champs Elysées (perfumes).

Paris chic – enviable, inimitable –
embodied by its women, its designers,
its models

Fashion

For most people, Paris fashion suggests a dreamworld of elegance, refinement, fantasy and originality that has helped to create the glamorous image of the French capital.

Only a few designers and creators belong to the exclusive club of *haute couture* whose very existence depends on the collections. These are feverishly prepared in great secrecy and revealed during ritual fashion shows in January and June for designer clothes, March and October for *prêt-à-porter* (ready-to-wear). The media play an essential role in these sophisticated 'performances', in which the top models are the stars. The designers create made-to-measure, very expensive outfits for a mainly foreign clientele. Behind the scenes, a whole army of *petites mains* (seamstresses), embroiderers, milliners, and so on, work endless hours to realise the masterpieces. The creators, on the other hand, concentrate their efforts on *prêt-à-porter*, accessories and perfumes, initiating new styles and trends that are copied by clothes manufacturers everywhere.

Well apart from the glittering world of designer clothes, the Sentier district (rue Réaumur and side streets, métro Sentier) houses a thousand or so stylists who are in direct contact with retail shops and who test a limited number of designs. They then mass-produce the most successful ones in the space of a few days.

Major projects are under consideration to consolidate the success of the lucrative but vulnerable fashion industry. A *maison de la mode* (headquarters of fashion) is being built under the place du Carrousel at the Louvre, and there are plans for a *cité internationale de la mode* near La Villette. However, above all, several specialised schools ensure that the young designers of tomorrow are being trained to follow in the footsteps of Cardin, Givenchy, Yves St-Laurent, Christian Dior, Chanel and a score of household names that have made Paris the world capital of fashion.

Entitertainment

*T*here are numerous opportunities for entertainment of every kind, whether cultural or not, for the whole family to enjoy or for adults only, by day or by night.

What's on

The Office du Tourisme et des Congrès de Paris brings out two publications: an annual one called *Saisons de Paris,* which lists the main events (festivals, exhibitions, concerts, etc); and the more detailed, monthly one, *Paris Sélection,* which has a special section devoted to young people, some useful addresses and shopping suggestions.

You can also ring **Paris Sélection Loisirs** (47 20 88 98) at any time of day or night to get pre-recorded weekly information in English.

Furthermore, there are two excellent weekly publications in French (both out on Wednesday) costing only a few francs, *Pariscope* and *l'Officiel des Spectacles.* They include up-to-date admission charges and a special listing of restaurants open after midnight.

Tickets

Tickets for the theatre, concerts and other shows can be obtained directly or from the agencies listed below, through which advance bookings can be made from abroad. This is strongly recommended as performances often become booked up very quickly.
Billetel, 6 boulevard de Sébastopol, 75004. Tel: 48 04 75 13. Fax: 42 74 30 69. Métro Châtelet.
Marais Spectacle, 15 rue aux Ours, 75003. Tel: 42 71 04 40. Fax: 42 71 18 16. Métro Rambuteau.
Agence Perrosier, 6 place de la Madeleine, 75008. Tel: 42 60 58 31. Fax: 42 60 14 83. Métro Madeleine.
Virgin Megastore, 52–60 Champs Elysées, 75008. Tel: 40 74 06 48. Fax: 42 56 52 60. Métro Franklin-Roosevelt.

Half-price tickets for performances the same day are available from the following kiosks:
15 place de la Madeleine, 75008. Open: Tuesday to Sunday 12.30pm–8pm. Métro Madeleine.
Inside the Châtelet-les-halles RER station, 75001. Open: Tuesday to Saturday 12.30pm–8pm.

Cinemas

Cinemas do well in Paris and film reviews are given extensive coverage in the weekly 'what's on' publications. There is always a good choice of new releases, called *exclusivités,* and of old films, called *reprises,* often shown *en version originale, v o* for short (in the original language), particularly on the Champs Elysées, in the Latin Quarter and Odéon district. Large cinemas have several auditoriums, each showing a different film; for instance, the George V at 144 and 146 avenue des Champs Elysées has no fewer than 11 auditoriums, the Gaumont Ambassade at no 50 has seven and there are several other multiple cinemas along the 'Champs' as well as three in the Forum des Halles.

Some cinemas go in for festivals

devoted to famous directors or actors: for instance, Hommage à Frank Capra, La Légende Bogart or Viva James Bond!

Classics are shown in the *cinémathèques* of the Palais de Chaillot and of the Palais de Tokyo (métro Trocadéro), as well as in the Centre Pompidou (métro Rambuteau), while the *vidéothèque* of the Forum des Halles (métro Les Halles) mainly shows documentaries.

In most cinemas prices are reduced on Mondays. On other days children, students and sometimes senior citizens are entitled to a reduction.

It is customary to tip usherettes.

Paris, city of cinematophiles

Theatres

The most prestigious of them all, the Comédie Française, also called le Théâtre Français or simply le Français (see page 98), traditionally puts on the great French classical comedies and tragedies by Molière, Racine, Corneille, Marivaux, Beaumarchais and Hugo. However, its repertoire now extends to selected 20th-century French and foreign plays. The acting is usually superb.

2 rue de Richelieu, 75001. Tel: 40 15 00 15. Métro Palais-Royal.

The following theatres put on interesting productions of French and foreign plays by mainly contemporary authors; booking usually starts two weeks in advance.

L'Atelier, place Charles-Dullin, 75018. Tel: 46 06 49 24. Métro Anvers.
Cartoucherie, route du Champ-des-Manoeuvres, 75012. Métro Château de Vincennes, then shuttle service. It comprises three theatres: Théâtre de la Tempête, tel: 42 28 36 36; Atelier du Chaudron, tel: 43 28 97 04 and Théâtre du Soleil, tel: 43 74 24 08.

Espace Critic (Espace Cardin), 3 avenue Gabriel, 75008. Tel: 42 64 37 33. Métro Concorde.
Espace Marais, 22 rue Beautreillis, 75004. Tel: 48 04 91 55. Métro St-Paul.
Hébertot, 78 bis boulevard des Batignolles, 75017. Tel: 43 87 23 23. Métro Villiers or Rome.
Huchette, 23 rue de la Huchette, 75005. Tel: 43 26 38 99. Métro St-Michel; the same plays by Eugene Ionesco have been on show here for ages.
Lucenaire Centre National d'Art et d'Essai, 53 rue Notre-Dame-des-Champs, 75006. Tel: 45 44 57 34. Métro Vavin.
Odéon Théâtre de l'Europe, place Paul Claudel, 75006. Tel: 43 25 70 32. Métro Odéon.
Renaud-Barrault, 1 bis avenue Franklin-Roosevelt, 75008. Tel: 42 56 60 70.
Théâtre National de Chaillot, 1 place du Trocadéro, 75016. Tel: 47 27 26 27. Métro Trocadéro.

Variety in an unpressured atmosphere: a leisurely petit déjeuner, a mid-morning pick-me-up, a range of hot options, an observation post on society

Café Life

The French café is an institution; it is not a bar, that is not subtle enough, it is not a pub, that is not Latin enough, it is not a wine bar either, although it does sell wine. In a word, the French café is unique. Most visitors to France know that, and their faces light up at the thought of indulging an hour or two sitting on the crowded terrace of a café, basking in the sun and watching the world go by.

Cafés are busy all day. They open early in the morning, in time to serve the traditional *grand crème* (large cup of white coffee) with *croissants* to people on their way to work. Throughout the day they serve wine by the glass, beer – *un demi* (originally 1/2 litre, just over a pint) or *une pression* (a glass of draught beer) – or *un pastis,* a strong aniseed drink diluted with water,

and, of course, the tiny *espresso,* a cup of strong black coffee that seems to keep French people going. Drinks are cheaper *au bar* (standing at the bar) than *en salle* (sitting at one of the typical round tables). You can always spot the *garçon* (waiter) with his black trousers, white shirt and black waistcoat, as he makes his way through the crowd with great agility.

The local cafés where 'regulars' have their drink at 11am, working people eat a quick snack at lunchtime and local residents meet in the evening to catch up on the news, play an important role in the city's social life. They have nothing in common with the elegant establishments of the place de l'Opéra, full of wealthy tourists and retired Parisians, or even with the Left Bank cafés where a fashionable élite goes to be seen!

Festivals

*F*estivals stem from an ancient tradition, but their number has greatly increased in recent years and they have developed from spontaneous regular gatherings into elaborate forms of entertainment aimed at occasional visitors as well as local residents.

FESTIVALS IN PARIS

Juin à Paris XVIe: During June, concerts, guided visits and plays are organised in churches, museums and the *mairie* of the 16th *arrondissement*. On 21 June there is an afternoon procession of horse-drawn carriages from the avenue Foch to the Auteuil racecourse.
For information tel: 45 03 21 16.

Festival 'Foire St-Germain': A different theme is chosen every year for this event, which takes place in June in the 6th *arrondissement* (St-Germain-des-Prés) and includes theatre, music, exhibitions and an antiques fair.
Venues: the Mairie, 78 rue Bonaparte, the place St-Sulpice, the Hôtel de la Monnaie, 11 quai de Conti. For information tel: 43 29 12 78.

Les Soirées de l'Hôtel d'Albret: Concerts of classical music, jazz and popular music during June.
31 rue des Francs-Bourgeois, 75004. For information tel: 42 33 43 00. Métro St-Paul.

Les Fêtes du Marais: This lively festival stages music, drama, exhibitions and outdoor festivities during June.
For information tel: 42 74 20 04.

Festival de la Butte Montmartre: In June and July theatre, music and dance bring life to various venues.
For information contact the tourist office: 42 62 46 22.

Festival Musique en l'Ile: During July and August, Ile St-Louis echoes with the sounds of classical music, oratorios and chamber music.
Eglise St-Louis-en-l'Ile, 19 bis rue St-Louis-en-l'Ile, 75004. Métro Pont-Marie. Some concerts take place on the Left Bank, in the church of St-Germain-des-Prés, place St-Germain-des-Prés, 75006. Métro St-Germain-des-Prés. For information tel: 40 30 10 13.

Paris, Quartier d'Eté: This is an indoor and outdoor festival of popular entertainment, with venues spread across the capital, from mid-July to mid-August.
For information tel: 40 28 40 33.

Festival Estival de Paris: From late July to early September, concerts of classical music are given in churches all over the city.
For information, tel: 48 04 98 01.

Festival d'Automne: From mid-September to the end of December, this festival stages music, dance, plays and special exhibitions in traditional venues such as theatres, museums and concert halls.
For information tel: 42 96 12 27.

Festival d'Art Sacré de la Ville de Paris: This festival of church music takes place in churches throughout October and November.
For information tel: 42 33 43 00.

Festival de jazz de Paris: Held in various halls from the end of October to the beginning of November.
For information tel: 47 83 84 06.

FESTIVALS IN ILE-DE-FRANCE

For information concerning the various events in the Paris region, contact the Comité Régional du Tourisme d'Ile-de-France, 73-75 rue Cambronne, 75015. Tel: 45 67 89 41.

St-Denis: A music festival in late May and June.

Versailles: The festival of instrumental music and opera holds performances in the Opéra Royal at the château, from the end of May until the end of June. The Grandes Fêtes de Nuit take place in the gardens in July, August and September.

Fontainebleau: Concerts are given in the castle during July and August.

Parc de Sceaux (RER Parc de Sceaux): From July until September, the Saison musicale d'été gives concerts in the Orangerie.

Abbaye de Royaumont: During May, June, September and October, concerts take place in the abbey buildings.

St-Germain-en-Laye: An international festival in honour of the composer Claude Debussy in September.

Suresnes (8km west of Paris): During the first weekend in October, a wine festival takes place to celebrate *les vendanges*.

Rueil-Malmaison: The Festival International du Film d'Histoire in November, is devoted to historical films.

FAIRS AND SPECIAL EVENTS

Foire du Trône: A funfair operates in the Bois de Vincennes, April and May.

Fête de la Musique: Events are staged in the 20 *arrondissements* of Paris on 21 June. *For information tel: 40 36 50 50.*

Nuit de la St-Jean: Impressive fireworks on 24 June, in the gardens of the Sacré-Coeur.

La Fête Nationale: A huge open-air ball on the place de la Bastille, on 13 July, followed by a military parade along the Champs Elysées on 14 July in the morning and fireworks in the evening at the Trocadéro.

Fête des Tuileries: An extensive funfair operates in the Tuileries gardens, from the beginning of July to mid-August and again in December.

Fête à Neu Neu: Another funfair, this time in the Bois de Boulogne, runs during September.

ART EXHIBITIONS

L'univers Fantasmagorique de Dali: A permanent exhibition devoted to Salvador Dali at Espace Montmartre, 11 rue Poulbot, 75018. Tel: 42 64 44 80. Open: 10am–7pm from October to March, 10am–10pm from April to September. Métro Abbesses or Anvers plus funicular.

Salon de Mars: Antiquities, primitive art, modern and contemporary art, at the end of March, on the Esplanade du Champ de Mars, 75007.

Les Cinq Jours de l'Objet Extraordinaire: A display of antiques in late May by dealers of the Carré Rive Gauche, 75007.

Foire Internationale d'Art Contemporain (FIAC): International contemporary art at the Grand Palais, avenue Winston Churchill, 75008. End of October. Métro Champs-Elysées Clémenceau.

Salon d'Automne: Paintings, sculptures, drawings, photographs and architecture also at the Grand Palais during the second half of October or the first half of November.

Salon des Artistes Indépendants: This art exhibition has a different theme every year; it follows the Salon d'Automne at the Grand Palais.

TRADE EXHIBITIONS

The Chambre de Commerce et d'Industrie de Paris, tel: 42 89 77 09, and the Fédération Française des Salons Spécialisés, tel: 42 25 05 80, publish a comprehensive list of trade exhibitions in Paris. Below is a selection.

Brocante de Paris: Antiques fair in early February at the Espace Champerret, Porte de Champerret, 75017. Métro Louise-Michel.

Foire à la Ferraille de Paris: Literally a 'scrap-iron fair', in fact an antiques fair held in February, May and September in the Parc Floral de Paris, Bois de Vincennes, 75012. Métro Château de Vincennes.

Musicora: This international exhibition of classical music is held during April in the Grand Palais, avenue Winston Churchill, 75008. Métro Champs-Elysées-Clémenceau.

Foire Internationale de Paris: Includes tourism, books, gardens, wines, sports and entertainment; in May at the Parc des Expositions de Paris, Porte de Versailles, 75015. Métro Porte de Versailles.

Mondial de l'Automobile: This motor-car show takes place every other year in October at the Parc des Expositions de Paris, see above.

Salon du Cheval et du Poney: All about horses, with various activities and showjumping, in December at the Parc des Expositions de Paris, see above.

Salon Nautique International: A very popular boat show, just before Christmas at the Parc des Expositions de Paris, see above.

MUSIC

As soon as the season ends in June, festivals take over so that there is always a wide choice of concerts.

Classical concerts

Paris has many orchestras, from the chamber ensemble to the symphony orchestra. The most prestigious are the Orchestre national de France, the Orchestre Philharmonique de Radio France, the Orchestre de Paris and the Ensemble Intercontemporain. The main venues vary in size from the small Salle Gaveau to the vast Théâtre des Champs Elysées and the Salle Pleyel. There are lunchtime or early evening concerts in many churches throughout the capital, concerts in parks and gardens from May to September, and a recently launched operation, *Monuments en Musique,* which provides short musical programmes at regular intervals in selected monuments.

Opera and ballet

Most major operas are now staged at the Opéra Bastille, but the Opéra Garnier seems to be getting its share again, when technical conditions permit. The rest of the time it is the exclusive home of ballet. The Orchestre de l'Opéra de Paris, which is shared between the two houses is one of the top orchestras in the country.

Jazz, rock and pop music

Concerts are usually held in large venues such as the new Zénith at La Villette (see page 114), the Palais Omnisports Paris Bercy, boulevard de Bercy, 75012, métro Bercy, and the Palais des Congrès, Porte Maillot, 75017. Métro Porte-Maillot. The old Olympia music-hall in the boulevard des Capucines, 75009, métro Opéra, is the traditional venue for variety shows and all aspiring artists hope to top the bill there.

Nightlife

Like most capital cities, Paris has a large

number of bars, discos, nightclubs and sex-shows (the latter mainly in the sleazy Pigalle area), but its cabaret shows are still considered as the most typically French form of night entertainment.

Cabarets

These became famous at the turn of the century partly for their lavish, colourful productions and partly because they shocked the predominantly bourgeois society. Today they no longer shock anyone, but their productions are just as lavish.

Moulin Rouge is probably the most famous with its 'girls' dancing the French Cancan in a frenzy of flying feathers; 82 Boulevard Clichy 75018, tel: 46 06 00 19. Other establishments include the **Folies Bergère**, 32 rue Richer, 75009, tel: 42 46 77 11, probably the most old-fashioned; the **Lido**, 116 bis avenue des Champs Elysées, 75008, tel: 45 63 11 61, with its sophisticated light effects; and the **Crazy Horse Saloon**, 12 avenue George V, 75008, tel: 47 23 32 32, reputed to be the most 'with it' of all.

Jazz clubs

Very popular at the moment, these are also very crowded; arrive early but don't expect things to get going before 11pm.
Caveau de la Huchette: One of the last authentic jazz cellars.
5 rue de la Huchette, 75005. Tel: 43 26 65 05. Métro St-Michel.
Louisiane: Real New-Orleans in an appropriate setting.
176 rue Montmartre, 75002. Tel: 45 08 95 02. Métro Montmartre.
New Morning: All the 'Greats' have played here, and tradition continues.
7 rue des Petites Ecuries, 75010. Tel: 45 23 51 41. Métro Château d'Eau.

Petit Journal: New Orleans and Dixie in a narrow vaulted cellar.
71 boulevard St-Michel, 75005. Tel: 43 26 28 59. Métro Luxembourg.
Sunset: Traditional jazz alternates with modern trends.
60 rue des Lombards, 75001. Tel: 40 26 46 60. Métro Châtelet.

Discos

These liven up from midnight onwards; trendy clothes are your best passport.
La Locomotive: A lot of space to dance to funk, urban rap and house music.
90 boulevard de Clichy, 75018. Tel 42 23 55 00. Métro Place de Clichy.
La Main Jaune: You can show off your roller-skating technique in this disco.
Rue Caporal Peugeot, 75017. Tel: 47 63 26 47.
Le Palace: Mixed crowds and theme nights have insured the lasting popularity of this reasonably priced disco.
8 rue du Faubourg-Montmartre, 75009. Tel: 42 46 10 87. Métro Rue-Montmartre.
La Scala: Special effects with laser lights create the mood.
188 bis rue de Rivoli, 75001. Tel: 42 61 64 00.

The famous Moulin Rouge

Children

*P*aris and the Ile-de-France offer children of all ages a choice of entertaining activities, whatever the weather.

MONUMENTS

A climb up the Eiffel Tower will thrill youngsters of all ages, while older ones will enjoy the Conciergerie and its gruesome stories, the Château de Vincennes and Versailles (the latter in small doses).

MUSEUMS

The Musée Grévin in the boulevard Montmartre with its wax figures of famous historical and contemporary characters is both entertaining and educational (see page 91).

Quite a few museums organise special activities for children of different age groups; the Cité des Sciences et de l'industrie at la Villette (see page 114), offers an introduction to science and technology called *l'Inventorium* with workshops for 3-to-6 and 6-to-12 year-olds; robots, computers and audio-visual games encourage children to participate and there are special shows at the planetarium.

The Centre Georges Pompidou (see page 52) aims to help children discover Art through workshops based on current exhibitions.

On Wednesday afternoons, at the Musée d'Orsay (see page 86), there are guided visits of the collections based on a theme as well as workshops for 5- to 10- year-olds.

The Palais de la Découverte (see page 37) has chemistry and astronomy workshops for teenagers.

In the Musée des Arts d'Afrique et d'Océanie (see page 121), there is a huge tropical aquarium with turtles, crocodiles and sharks, which never fails to impress children.

Enter the world of Jacques Cousteau

The world of the sea

At the Parc Océanique Cousteau in the Forum des Halles, children (and adults) embark on an exploration of the deep sea world with the help of the latest audio-visual techniques and discover a stunning environment of coral reefs and volcanoes with strange animals and dense forests of giant seaweeds.

Forum des Halles, 75001. Tel: 40 26 13 78. Open: Tuesday and Thursday 10am–4pm, Wednesday, Friday and weekends 10am–5.30pm. Admission charge. Métro Les Halles.

Centre de la Mer et des Eaux: At this marine and freshwater centre, simple phenomena are explained through observation, games and audio-visual presentations.

195 rue St-Jacques, 75005. Tel: 46 33 08 61. Open 10am–12.30pm and

1.15pm–5.30pm. Closed: Monday.
Admission charge. Métro Luxembourg.

PARKS AND GARDENS

The Jardin d'Acclimatation in the Bois de Boulogne is an amusement park for children of all ages with roundabouts, pony rides, a miniature farm, a mini-golf course and an enchanted river. A little train runs a shuttle service between the Porte Maillot and the park on Wednesday, Saturday and Sunday afternoons and during school holidays.
Bois de Boulogne, 75016. Tel: 40 67 90 82. Open 10am–6pm. Admission charge. Métro Porte Maillot (little train) or Sablons.

The Jardin des Enfants at Les Halles is an adventure playground for 7- to 11-year-olds, complete with jungle, volcano and lost city.
105 rue Rambuteau, 75003. Tel: 45 08 07 18. Métro les Halles.

Most parks in the capital have a children's play area. Three, however, are better equipped. The Parc des Buttes-Chaumont (see page 138) has lots of space and plenty of attractions including rock-climbing for older children. The Parc Georges Brassens (see page 138) has wooden huts in a miniature forest setting with rocks to match, as well as the usual attractions. The Parc Floral de Paris in the Bois de Vincennes (see page 121) aims to initiate children in the pleasures of a nature trail.

ZOOS

There is a small zoo in the Jardin des Plantes (see page 138) and another in the Bois de Vincennes (see page 121).

FUN WITH WATER

Aquaboulevard is an adventure playground in an aquatic environment, and offers such attractions as giant slides and a bubble pool.
5 rue Louis-Armand, 75015. Tel: 40 60 15 15. Open 9am–11pm. Admission charge. Métro Balard.

In fine weather, children will enjoy a boat trip on the Lac Inférieur in the Bois de Boulogne or on the Lac Daumesnil in the Bois de Vincennes, and will be fascinated by a trip on the Seine in one of the *bateau-mouches* (see page 187).

The perfect match: kids and open space

SHOWS

There are *Guignol* (Punch and Judy) shows in most public parks and gardens including the Luxembourg and Tuileries gardens, and those listed above.

Paris also has a number of circuses which sometimes move about according to the season. Below is a list of those you can ring for the latest information on performances:
Cirque Bouglione, tel: 47 00 12 25.
Cirque Franconi, tel: 43 24 33 18.
Cirque Pauwels, tel: 40 67 90 82.
Cirque Zavatta, tel: 42 81 35 95.

Sport

*R*egular television coverage of sports events has contributed to a change of attitude towards sport in France, and particularly in Paris. Sport has entered every home, and the number of spectators has reached phenomenal proportions. This has had two direct consequences: more money has been invested in making sport accessible to a wider public; and stadiums and large indoor venues have been modernised and enlarged, and facilities for individual sports have been improved, while new ones have been created. Moreover, participation in sporting activities is now widely considered to be a good way of relieving the stress of modern city life, and keeping fit. Therefore, a new range of activities, formerly reserved for professionals, are gradually being made available to the public at large.

The Prix de l'Arc de Triomphe, Longchamp

SPORT CENTRES AND STADIUMS

More than 500 national and international sports events take place every year in the city's main venues.

Built in 1984, the **Palais Omnisports de Paris-Bercy** is a huge multi-purpose centre where 150 different events take place annually, from cycling competitions to showjumping, rock-climbing and boxing. The seating capacity is adapted to each event, with a maximum of 17,000. There is also an ice-skating rink, numerous dressing-rooms and a medical centre. In addition, the Palais Omnisports is frequently used for rock concerts.
8 boulevard de Bercy, 75012. Tel: 43 41 72 04. Métro Bercy.

With a capacity of 50,000 spectators, the **Parc des Princes** is the main venue for football and rugby matches. It is situated in an affluent residential district just south of the Bois de Boulogne.
24 rue du Commandant-Guilbaud, 75016. Tel: 42 88 02 76. Métro Exelmans or Porte de St-Cloud.

Quite close is the famous **Stade Roland-Garros**, a tennis complex with 16 courts, including a centre court with room for 16,500 spectators. Plans for extension are under study.
2 avenue Gordon-Bennett, 75016. Tel: 47 43 48 00. Métro Porte d'Auteuil.

Next to it, on the edge of the Bois de Boulogne, are two of the capital's three racecourses: the **Hippodrome d'Auteuil**, place de la Porte d'Auteuil, tel: 45 27 12 25, métro Porte d'Auteuil, famous for steeplechasing, and the **Hippodrome de Longchamp**, boulevard Anatole-France, tel: 45 20 08 88, métro Porte d'Auteuil. The third racecourse is the Hippodrome de Vincennes, on the other side of town. Entrance 2 route de la Ferme, 75012. Tel: 49 77 17 17. RER Joinville-le-Pont.

Still in the 16th *arrondissement*, the Stade Pierre de Coubertin stages around 100 events such as judo and fencing competitions, gymnastics and dance displays, boxing and basket-ball matches, for the benefit of 5,000 spectators.
82 avenue Georges-Lafont, 75016. Tel: 45 27 79 12. Métro Porte de St-Cloud.

The Stade Georges Carpentier, with a similar capacity, has also been renovated recently and holds indoor sports competitions such as martial arts, volley-ball, badminton and table tennis.
81 boulevard Masséna, 75013. Tel: 45 85 57 43. Métro Porte d'Ivry or Porte de Choisy.

When it opens in 1994, the vast new Stade Charléty, with a capacity of 20,000 spectators, will host both outdoor and indoor sports, from football and rugby to athletics, squash and tennis.
1 avenue de la porte de Gentilly, 75013. Métro Cité Universitaire.

Built for the 1924 Olympic Games, the Georges Vallerey swimming-pool saw Johnny Weissmüller of Tarzan fame beat the world 400m freestyle record. Entirely modernised in 1989, it can now hold water polo competitions as well as international swimming contests.
148 avenue Gambetta, 75020. Tel: 40 31 15 20. Métro Porte des Lilas.

CALENDAR OF MAIN EVENTS

Cycling: The colourful and often dramatic finish of the *Tour de France* is staged along the Champs Elysées.

Football: The *Coupe de France* is held in the Parc des Princes in April or May.

Racing: Several famous races attract the crowds at the city's three racecourses: the *Prix d'Amérique* at Vincennes in January, the *Prix du Président de la République* at Auteuil on Palm Sunday, the *Grand Steeple Chase de Paris* at Auteuil on the third Sunday in June and the *Grand Prix de Paris* at Longchamp a week later, and the *Grand Prix de l'Arc de Triomphe* at Longchamp in early October.

Rugby: The *Tournoi des Cinq Nations*, involving England, Scotland, Wales, Ireland and France is held at the Parc des Princes.

Running: The famous *Marathon de Paris* takes place in the capital in March or April.

Tennis: The *Championnats Internationaux de France* (French Open) take place at the Stade Roland-Garros in late May and early June.

The *Open de la Ville de Paris* is held in the Palais Omnisports de Paris-Bercy in late October.

The French Open at Stade Roland-Garros

Sport

*T*here are more than 250 locations all over Paris where amateurs and professionals can practise the sport of their choice. Municipal equipment is available to everyone for a very modest fee, and visitors may join certain private clubs on a temporary basis. Certain activities can easily be pursued in town, others need open space.

SPORTS FACILITIES IN PARIS

Tennis and swimming are the most popular sports, while an increasing number of fitness clubs with sophisticated equipment are appearing on the scene. However, you can also go in for riding, martial arts, skating, squash, canoeing, diving and rock-climbing; and you can even keep your hand at golf without leaving the city.

To get the best information on what is available in your area, contact the Office Municipal des Sports in the *mairie d'arrondissement* (district town hall). You can also obtain from the *mairie* a booklet entitled *Centre d'Animation Magazine,* published twice yearly which contains a list of all sports centres with addresses and programmes. *Sport à la carte* has been specially devised to provide individual programmes in municipal centres at fixed hours.

Bowling

This has been popular with young people for some time, more as a leisure activity than a sport.
Bowling Champerret, place Porte Champerret, 75017. Tel: 43 80 24 64. Open: daily 10am–2am. Bar. Métro Porte de Champerret.
Bowling Foch, 8 avenue Foch, 75016. Tel: 45 00 00 13. Open: daily 11am–2am. Bar. Métro Etoile.
Bowling Montparnasse, 27 rue Commandant-Mouchotte, 75014. Tel: 43 21 61 32. Open: daily 10am–2am (4am on Friday and Saturday). Bar-restaurant. Métro Montparnasse.

Climbing

Three new structures have been installed in the city to accommodate the growing number of enthusiasts; the most impressive is located at the **Stade des Poissonniers**, 2 rue Jean-Cocteau, 75018. Tel: 42 51 24 68. Open: Wednesday 2.30pm–5pm. Maximum height: 21m. Métro Porte de Clignancourt.

For other possibilities and information contact the **Fédération Française de la Montagne et de l'Escalade**, 20 bis rue de la Boétie, 75008. Tel: 47 42 39 80.

Cycling

Nearly 400 clubs in the Paris region organise tours in Ile-de-France. For information, contact one of the following:

Comité d'Ile-de-France de la Fédération Fraçaise du Cyclisme, 7 rue Darboy, 75011. Tel: 43 57 02 94. Fédération Française de Cyclisme, 43 rue de Dunkerque, 75010. Tel: 42 85 41 20. Fédération Française de Cyclotourisme, 8 rue Jean-Marie-Jégo, 75013. Tel: 45 80 30 21.

Golf

Several clubs and centres offer golfers the possibility of practising their putting, and even their drive, with the help of simulators. However, the real thing takes place out of town. For detailed information, contact the Fédération Française de Golf, 69 avenue Victor-Hugo, 75016. Tel: 45 02 13 55.

Gymnastics and fitness

Many clubs specialise in keep-fit classes, aerobics, body-building, swimming and so on. They are equipped with saunas and jacuzzis and usually work on membership. One of the most sophisticated is Espace Vit'Halles, 48 rue Rambuteau, 75003. Tel: 42 77 21 71. Métro Rambuteau.

Swimming

There are many municipal swimming-pools in Paris and a number of private ones. The following is a selection of the most attractive:

Piscine Deligny: a floating pool along the quai Anatole-France, 75007. Tel: 45 51 72 15. Métro Solférino.

Piscine Jean Taris: lovely Japanese

Left: Cycling in the Bois de Boulogne

garden setting. 16 rue Thouin, 75005. Tel: 43 25 54 03. Métro Cardinal-Lemoine.

Piscine des Halles: an olympic-size pool with a view of the tropical glasshouse. Forum des Halles. Tel: 42 36 98 44. Métro Les Halles.

Tennis and squash

There are 150 municipal tennis courts open until 10pm, available by the hour at very reasonable fees. For detailed information, contact the local *mairie* or Allo Sport (see the **Practical Guide, Sport**).

In addition, there are several private clubs:

Squash Montmartre: four courts, clubhouse, restaurant. 14 rue Achille Martinet, 75018. Tel: 42 55 38 30. Métro Lamarck.

Squash-Golf Rennes Raspail: seven courts and golf practice. 149 rue de Rennes, 75006. Tel: 45 44 24 35. Métro Rennes.

Tennis de Longchamp: 20 courts. 19 boulevard Anatole-France, 92 Boulogne. Tel: 46 03 84 49. Métro Porte d'Auteuil.

Water-skiing, canoeing, etc

This is now possible at the new **Bassin de la Villette**, 5 bis quai de la Loire, 75019. Métro Jaurès or Stalingrad.

Leisure parks outside Paris

Activities include swimming, sailing, wind-surfing, canoeing, riding and tennis.

Parc de Loisirs Torcy Marne-la-Vallée, route de Lagny, 77 Torcy. 25km (15 miles) east of Paris. Tel: 64 80 58 75. RER Torcy-Marne-la-Vallée. Open: 9am–7pm.

Le Val de Seine, 78480 Verneuil-sur-Seine. 30km (18 miles) west of Paris. Tel: 39 71 07 06. Open: 10am–7pm.

Food and Drink

*F*ood is an important ingredient of the French way of life and some of the rituals that accompany its preparation and consumption are still performed by a majority of French people, even in Paris where the pressures of modern city life seem to go against the more traditional principles of gastronomy.

Eating habits

One thing the French are particular about is 'fresh' food: bread, meat and vegetables are usually bought daily. A lot of people shop after working hours, which explains why food shops and markets stay open late. The time spent on cooking varies, but has been considerably shortened for working people, thanks to the mouth-watering, freshly prepared dishes sold in the numerous *charcuteries*. The traditional three-course meal (dessert being optional) often ends on a generous helping of cheese.

Although French people still have two main meals a day, around midday and 8pm, in Paris lunch tends to be reduced to a quick light meal, the emphasis being on the evening meal served with wine. A family meal generally consists of one type of wine, usually red, while special meals include at least two different wines, carefully chosen to go with each dish. Some people drink beer with their meals, and nearly everyone drinks mineral water and fruit juice some time during the day. Breakfast is not very copious: freshly bought bread with butter and jam, marmalade or honey, and/or a *croissant*. *Boulangeries* open early so people can drop in for fresh supplies before going to work. *Café au lait* or *café crème* (white coffee) as it is called in cafés, is still the

Takeaway food in a class by itself

traditional breakfast drink, but more people drink black coffee these days, and tea is gaining in popularity.

Shopping for food

Food shops have a place of honour in the best districts, and some of them have elaborate, imaginative displays worthy of shops selling luxury goods, for that is exactly what they are doing. It is a pleasure just to window-shop along the specialised streets or to browse round the colourful markets. However, having enjoyed French cuisine, you will certainly want to know more about it, and perhaps take a speciality home with you.

Shopping streets and markets

Each district has an open-air market as well as one or two streets, often pedestrianised during part of the day, where food shops are concentrated and stalls are set up on the pavement to promote certain kinds of produce. Prices can vary considerably, but the accent is on friendliness and customers are invited to select what they want. Basic shops always include one or two *boucheries* (butchers), *boulangeries-pâtisseries* (bakers), *crémeries-fromageries* (dairies), *charcuteries* (delicatessens) and *poissonneries* (fishmongers).

The following streets are renowned for good quality and good value.

Near Les Halles: the rue Montorgueil, which still keeps alive the atmosphere of the old central food market (see page 66), and the rue Rambuteau.

In the 17th *arrondissement:* the rue Poncelet near the place des Ternes, where there is one of the best coffee shops in Paris, the Brûlerie des Ternes at no 10, and the rue de Lévis near the Parc Monceau.

On the Left Bank: the rue Mouffetard, the rue de Buci and the rue de Seine, probably the most picturesque in Paris.

Specialised shops

Cheese can be bought in supermarkets, *épiceries* (grocers) and from market stalls, but connoisseurs prefer to select from one of the 300 different cheeses made in France at a reputed *fromager*, who can recommend the best *brebis* (ewe's milk cheese) or the tastiest *chevrotin* (goat's milk cheese from Savoie) or a superb *Pont-l'Evêque* (a famous cow's milk cheese from Normandy).
Androuet, 41 rue d'Amsterdam, 75008, métro Liège, is something of a legend with over 200 varieties kept at the right temperature in the cellars.

Lionel Poilâne, 8 rue du Cherche-Midi, 75006, métro Sèvres-Babylone, an adept at authenticity, is undoubtedly the most famous baker in Paris, while the pâtisserie Lenôtre, 49 avenue Victor-Hugo, 75016, métro Victor-Hugo, is unequalled for imagination and refinement.
Berthillon, 31 rue St-Louis-en-l'Ile, 75004, métro Pont-Marie, is the best place for ice-cream, and has some unusual flavours.

The Madeleine area (métro Madeleine) has several luxury food shops, including the famous Fauchon, 26 place de la Madeleine, an *épicerie fine* (luxury grocer) and delicatessen whose displays are real works of art, and the more modest Hédiard at no 21. Next door at no 19 is the **Maison de la Truffe**, where you can buy fresh truffles as well as delicious *charcuterie.* Near by, in the rue Vignon, is the **Maison du Miel**, at no 24, where you can taste and buy all kinds of rare honey.

Goat's milk cheese in its many forms

Cuisine

It is a well known, although controversial fact that 'Paris is not France'; the French themselves acknowledge it, especially when they are not Parisians. Yet, paradoxically, although there is no Parisian cuisine as such, Paris has become a melting-pot of the best culinary traditions and the undisputed capital of French gastronomy.

Variety is the first and foremost characteristic of French cuisine. The ingredients used in cooking have regional origins; cream, butter and cheese are widely used in northern areas where milk products are plentiful, while olive oil and garlic are typical of Mediterranean areas and red wine makes casseroles rich and tasty in the Bourgogne district.

The universal fame of traditional French cuisine rests on various regional dishes, which now appear on typical menus everywhere.

Among starters, you may find *hors-d'oeuvre variés* (raw vegetables seasoned with oil and vinegar served with assorted *charcuterie*), *quiche lorraine* (savoury flan with pieces of bacon), *moules marinière* (mussels simmered in white wine with shallots), or the delicious *soupe à l'onion gratinée* (onion soup with melted cheese).

Main dishes usually include several of the following: *entrecôte bordelaise* (juicy steak with a rich wine sauce), *boeuf bourguignon* (casseroled beef with onions and mushrooms in a red Burgundy wine), *blanquette de veau* (stewed veal with cream and mushrooms) and *choucroute garnie* (sauerkraut cooked in dry white wine, with pork and sausages). *Gratin dauphinois* (sliced potatoes baked with cream and grated cheese) is ideal with tasty grills.

To finish a good meal, there is nothing more refreshing than a home-baked *crème caramel* (egg custard coated with caramel) or a cool *baba-au-rhum* (light sponge cake with rum syrup).

However, French cuisine does not rely for its success on tradition alone, for it is constantly being re-invented and perfected by ambitious young chefs whose imagination has no bounds.

Variety and quality are essential components of traditional French cuisine

Eating Out

Casual al fresco dining in Montmartre

The choice is vast and there are places to suit every occasion, from the local, inexpensive *bistro* to the exclusive temple of gastronomy, from fast-food bars and quaint tea-rooms to regional and exotic ethnic restaurants.

Each type of establishment has its own personality and represents a different aspect of Parisian life. Crowded at lunchtime, cafés are ideal for a quick meal, with a restricted menu usually consisting of *steak/frites* (steak and chips), mixed salads, and a selection of sandwiches made with crisp *baguettes* (French bread). Slightly more expensive, brasseries offer a choice of traditional dishes that includes an Alsatian *choucroute garnie* (sauerkraut with assorted sausages) served with beer or wine. Top brasseries have an attractive display of fresh seafood just outside their premises with an attendant serving oysters and other pricy delicacies to passers-by and preparing orders for customers inside. There are several such establishments on the place de Clichy, not far from the Moulin Rouge.

Wine bars are not steeped in tradition like cafés and brasseries, but they seem to fit in well with the Parisians' changing lifestyle and they are becoming increasingly popular as a lunchtime venue. They serve an assortment of cold platters and cheese with selected wines by the glass, thus enabling the real amateur to taste and enjoy excellent wine without having to buy a full bottle. L'Ecluse, 15 Quai des Grands-Augustins, 75006, métro St-Michel, is one of the most famous and a good place to sample for atmosphere.

Little known or talked about are the discreet but charming *salons de thé* (tea-rooms), often tucked away in picturesque arcades. They offer the luxury of a relaxed atmosphere in refined surroundings and serve good-quality snacks and pastries with a choice of fine teas or coffee. Two of the best are: Fanny-Tea, 20 place Dauphine, on the Ile-de-la-Cité, and La Cour de Rohan, Cour du Commerce St-André, off the rue St-André-des-Arts, near the place St-Michel.

The name restaurant applies to a wide range of establishments, from the unassuming, friendly, local place with white lace curtains at the windows and rickety tables outside in summertime to the select, fashionable, outrageously expensive or just exquisitely refined rendezvous for gourmets. The variety stems from the type of cuisine served, whether French or ethnic.

Paris is a real gold mine for French cuisine, with an infinite number of variations being offered on three main themes: traditional, modern and regional (see pages 166–7). Some restaurants combine traditional and modern methods.

Typical cuisines from the regions of France, on the other hand, are well represented by authentic chefs who have come to the capital to make a name for themselves. In some cases they are concentrated in a specific area. For instance, exponents of Breton cuisine are grouped in the vicinity of the Gare Montparnasse, while specialities from the Auvergne are to be found in the Bastille area.

The number of ethnic restaurants has increased lately and they, too, tend to congregate in specific areas, sometime taking over a whole street, like the rue de la Huchette, near the place St-Michel, lined with cheap Greek and North African restaurants. The rue des Rosiers and adjacent streets in the Marais are well known for their Jewish and East European restaurants and the 13th *arrondissement,* near the Porte d'Ivry, where Asian restaurants are plentiful, has been christened 'Chinatown'. By contrast, you hardly notice the less conspicuous presence of several Japanese restaurants in the Opéra district

Choosing a restaurant

It is difficult to generalise about value for money as quality and prices vary a lot. On the whole, however, one may say that, in the lower price range, value for money – both in quantity and quality – is better in Paris than in most Western capitals. This tends to be less true in the upper price range, but Paris still retains a slight advantage as far as service, attention to detail and imagination is concerned.

The price range given in the listings below refers to an average meal per person, not including drinks. There are four categories: less than 200 francs (F), from 200 to 300 francs (FF), from 300 to 500 francs (FFF), over 500 francs (FFFF). Wine with your meal can cost from around 60 francs a bottle to several hundred francs for a château wine.

Most restaurants offer a fixed menu (some at lunchtime only) which is better value for money than *à la carte* (chosen from the larger selection of dishes). In any case, a 15 per cent service charge is usually included in the price.

The restaurants selected are located in nine areas of particular interest, described in the 'What to see' section.

Rabbit, anyone? Lapin Agile, Montmartre

Restaurants

MARAIS, ILE ST-LOUIS
FFFF L'Ambroisie
Superb cuisine and refined décor, reservations essential.
9 place des Vosges, 75004. Tel: 42 78 51 45. Métro Bastille.
F Le Maraîcher
Imaginative cuisine; excellent value for money.
5 rue Beautreillis, 75004. Tel: 42 71 42 49. Métro Bastille.
F Nos Ancêtres les Gaulois
Four courses for a fixed price, unlimited wine included.
39 rue St-Louis-en-l'Ile, 75004. Tel: 46 33 66 07. Métro Pont-Marie,
FF Wally
One of the best North African restaurants in Paris.
16 rue Le Regrattier, 75004. Tel: 43 25 01 39. Métro Pont-Marie.

LES HALLES
F Au Pied de Cochon
Serves traditional onion soup.
6 rue Coquillière, 75001. Tel: 42 36 11 75. Métro Les Halles.
FF Chez Benoît
The typical atmosphere of an old-fashioned Parisian bistro.
20 rue St-Martin, 75004. Tel: 42 72 25 76. Métro Châtelet.

Waiting to serve you with French flair

FFF Gérard Besson
Authentic gourmet cuisine; elegant, comfortable décor.
5 rue Coq-Héron, 75001. Tel: 42 33 14 74. Métro Louvre.
F Le Dieu Gambrinus
Stunning, 13th-century beer cellar.
62 rue des Lombards, 75001. Tel: 42 21 10 30. Métro Les Halles.

PALAIS-ROYAL, OPÉRA, CONCORDE
F La Cave Drouot
Specialities from the Basque country.
8 rue Drouot, 75009. Tel: 47 70 83 38. Métro Richelieu-Drouot.
FF Le Grand Café Capucines
One of the top brasseries, serving excellent seafood.
4 boulevard des Capucines, 75009. Tel: 47 42 19 00. Métro Opéra.
FFFF Lucas-Carton
Superb cuisine supervised by one of Paris's top chefs.
9 place de la Madeleine, 75008. Tel: 42 65 22 90. Métro Madeleine.
FFFF Maxim's
Probably the most prestigious restaurant in Paris, reservations essential.
3 rue Royale, 75008. Tel: 42 65 27 94. Métro Concorde.

ETOILE, CHAMPS ELYSÉES
FFF Le Fouquet's
Rendezvous of film stars and celebrities.
99 avenue des Champs-Elysées, 75008. Tel: 47 23 70 60. Métro George V.
FF La Fermette Marbeuf
Fashionable but unpretentious restaurant, excellent low-priced menu in the evening.
5 rue Marbeuf, 75008. Tel: 47 20 63 53. Métro Alma-Marceau.
F Le Lyonnais
Specialities from the Lyon region.
26 rue d'Armaillé, 75017. Tel: 45 72 00 82. Métro Argentine.
FFFF Taillevent
Situated in a 19th-century mansion, offering traditional high-class cuisine.
15 rue Lamennais, 75008. Tel: 45 61 12 90. Métro George V.

Watching the world go by from the pavement

TROCADÉRO, PASSY

FFFF Jamin
Elegant cosy surroundings, cuisine inspired by a great chef.
32 rue de Longchamp, 75016. Tel: 47 27 12 27. Métro Trocadéro.

F Au Cadre Vert
Pleasant décor, traditional cuisine.
4 rue Lekain, 75016. Tel: 42 88 78 77. Métro La Muette.

F Au Rendez-Vous de Longchamp
Grilled meat and pastries are specialities.
79 avenue Kléber, 75016. Tel: 47 27 87 58. Métro Kléber.

MONTMARTRE

F Au Petit Moulin
One of the old cafés of Montmartre.
17 rue Tholozé, 75018. Tel: 42 52 42 16. Métro Abbesses.

FF Le Closdenis
Tasty cuisine from Provence.
57 rue Caulaincourt, 75018. Tel: 46 06 20 26. Métro Lamarck-Caulaincourt.

F Le Restaurant
In a quiet street of old Montmartre, imaginative cuisine.
32 rue Véron, 75018. Tel: 42 23 06 22. Métro Abbesses.

LATIN QUARTER

FFF Dodin Bouffant
Seafood a speciality.
25 rue Frédéric-Sauton, 75005. Tel: 43 25 25 14. Métro Maubert-Mutualité.

FF L'Atelier de Maître Albert
Fixed-price menu including half a bottle of wine.
1 rue Maître-Albert, 75005. Tel: 46 33 06 44. Métro Maubert-Mutualité.

FFFF La Tour d'Argent
Perfect cuisine, very expensive.
15 quai de la Tournelle, 75005. Tel: 43 54 23 31. Métro Maubert-Mutualité.

F Le Grenier Notre-Dame
Vegetarian restaurant very close to Notre-Dame.
18 rue de la Bûcherie, 75005. Tel: 43 29 98 29. Métro Maubert-Mutualité.

ST-GERMAIN-DES-PRÉS

F Aux Charpentier
Traditional publishers' haunt, tables outside in summer.
10 rue Mabillon, 75006. Tel: 43 26 30 05. Métro Mabillon.

FFF Jacques Cagna
Magnificent 17th-century house and excellent traditional cuisine.
14 rue des Grands-Augustins, 75006. Tel: 43 26 49 39. Métro St-Michel.

FF La Luna
Spanish cuisine with the emphasis on fish.
12 rue Dauphine, 75006. Tel: 46 33 85 85. Métro Odéon.

FF Le Petit Zinc
Typical Left Bank bistro serving excellent seafood.
25 rue de Buci, 75006. Tel: 46 33 51 66. Métro Mabillon.

F Polidor
Authentic bistro, convivial atmosphere.
41 rue Monsieur-le-Prince, 75006. Tel: 43 26 95 34. Métro Luxembourg.

INVALIDES, FAUBOURG ST-GERMAIN

F La Petite Chaise
Excellent value for money.
36 rue de Grenelle, 75007. Tel: 42 22 13 35, Métro Sèvres-Babylone.

FFFF Le Divellec
One of the top seafood restaurants.
107 rue de l'Université, 75007. Tel: 45 51 91 96. Métro Invalides.

FF Vin sur Vin
Close to the Eiffel Tower, friendly atmosphere, copious savoury dishes.
20 rue de Monttessuy, 75007. Tel: 47 05 14 20, Métro Pont de l'Alma.

Le Montagnard in Montmartre

Wine

Wine is the French national drink, its infinite variety matching that of French cuisine. Vines have been grown in France since Roman times, and ancestral traditions are still observed in many regions. Wine-making methods are strictly controlled and a grading system is applied accordingly.

Vin de table is a cheap, ordinary wine. It is drunk 'young' (within a year). Next comes the **Vin délimité de qualité supérieure (VDQS)**, a higher-grade wine produced in areas where quality is constant. **Appellation d'Origine Contrôlée (AOC)**, denotes a wine characteristic of a specific district, or *cru,* such as Médoc in the Bordeaux region.

This information and more is on the labels and it is well worth studying them carefully when selecting a good red or white château wine. Look for the year, as quality varies from year to year, and for the words *mis en bouteilles au château* (bottled at the château); but bear in mind that there are many château wines and the best of them have been graded as *cru bourgeois* and *grand cru* or *1er cru, 2ème cru,* and so on.

The two main wine-producing regions are the Bordeaux region in the southwest with famous wines like Médoc, Graves, St-Emilion or Pomerol and Bourgogne in the east, with inspiring names such as Nuits-St-Georges, Chambertin, Pommard and Pouilly-Fuissé.

Other regions also produce some great wines, for instance Châteauneuf-du-Pape, which comes from the Rhône valley, and Riesling from the Alsace.

Champagne is in a class of its own. The lengthy production process was perfected in the 17th century by Dom Pérignon, a monk who came from the abbaye d'Hautvillers.

Wine-bottle shapes vary from one region to another: providing an immediate clue to their origins. Thus the elegant slim bottle from the southwest contrasts with the stockier type used in Bourgogne and Champagne, or the tall fluted ones typical of Alsace.

Whatever your taste, your budget or the occasion, there's a bottle of wine to suit

Hotel Tips

*O*ld and new, traditional and modern, Parisian hotels vary considerably in size and the degree of comfort they offer. During the last few years, many have been renovated, modernised and refurbished with the emphasis on proper separate bathroom facilities instead of the usual wash-basin and bidet, even in the lowest grade. Only the more expensive hotels have restaurants.

Grading

The system used is the same as in other regions of France. Hotels are graded by the Direction de l'Industrie Touristique, according to the degree of comfort available and the quality of service offered. Present standards were fixed by decree in 1986 and regular checks are carried out by the Préfecture. There are five grades, which can be described as follows, starting with the lowest:

HT, HRT or ⋆ applies to modest hotels with basic comforts, but bear in mind that standards have risen recently, although not necessarily everywhere.

Comfort and convenience at a Left Bank hotel, one of over 1,400 throughout the city

** denotes a comfortable hotel, where you can expect a private bathroom.

*** qualifies a very comfortable hotel, where a private bathroom and toilet are standard and breakfast is served in the rooms if you so wish.

**** are granted to high-class hotels. Some have long been internationally famous: the Ritz, place Vendôme, 75001; the Crillon, place de la Concorde, 75008; the George V, avenue George V, 75008; and the Hilton International Paris, avenue de Suffren, 75015.

L**** is granted to only a very few de luxe hotels that the French call *palaces*. The Meurice, rue de Rivoli, 75001, was the German headquarters during World War II.

As they are in greater demand, there are more two- and three-star hotels throughout the city.

Breakfast

As a rule, all hotels provide breakfast, but generally only three-star and above offer room service. The price of breakfast is quoted separately from that of the room and you are not obliged to have it, although you may not be very popular in it you don't.

In most cases, hotels offer a 'continental' breakfast, which usually includes tea, milk, coffee or chocolate, a *baguette* (crisp French bread) with butter and jam or honey, and one or two *croissants*.

Some hotels now offer an English or American style breakfast customers on payment of a supplement.

Prices

By western standards, Parisian hotels are fairly reasonably priced on the whole, although they are more expensive than in French provincial towns. Charging by the room rather than per person is still common practice, which means that it is much cheaper for people to travel together (some hotels have family rooms for parents with one or two children).

Prices are not controlled and so vary a lot according to the time of year and even from one hotel to another, within a given official category; they can also be changed without prior notice. However, prices including tax and service charge must be displayed outside hotels, in the reception area and in the rooms.

The easiest method of payment is by credit card, which only a few hotels in the lowest category do not accept.

Selecting a hotel

Most people prefer central areas in order to reduce travelling times to a minimum and fully enjoy the atmosphere of the city. Most luxury hotels are in the Madeleine-Opéra-Champs Elysées area, which covers the 1st, 8th and 9th *arrondissements*, while the Left Bank, especially the 5th, 6th and 7th *arrondissements*, has a profusion of smaller, more relaxed, but still very comfortable, establishments. This is only a general indication and it is quite possible to find a middle- or lower-grade hotel on the Right Bank. Although they might seem convenient, some areas are best avoided: the Gare du Nord/Gare de l'Est area and eastern districts in general, and the red light district of Pigalle.

Once you have picked an area, you can make a list of suitable hotels using a free booklet published by the Office du Tourisme et des Congrès de Paris. You can obtain it by applying to the official representative of the French tourist office in your country (for addresses, see the Practical Guide, Tourist Offices).

Booking a Hotel

*I*t is advisable to book in advance (preferably a month or so) all the year round, but especially between Easter and October when more tourists come to Paris. You can do so by telephone, letter or fax. There are several points you should make quite clear: if the hotel is on a main street, ask for a room at the back, so that you are not disturbed by traffic noise; if it is a one- or two-star hotel, ask whether the room has a separate bathroom and, if you don't like climbing stairs, inquire whether there is a lift or ask for a room on a lower floor. Lastly, check the price. You will normally be expected to send a deposit with your confirmation.

If you arrive in Paris without having made a reservation, the Office du Tourisme et des Congrès de Paris will be able to help you: they have a *Service de Réservations Hôtelières* in their main offices which are located at 127 Champs Elysées, 75008 Paris, tel: 47 23 61 72, and are open daily from 9am to 8pm, and subsidiary offices at the main stations (except the Gare St-Lazare) as well as at the Eiffel Tower (from May to September only).

These act as an emergency service for immediate accommodation but they are closed on Sunday except at the Gare du Nord.

Below is a list of other organisations, *centrales de réservations hôtelières,* which deal with hotel bookings by phone or fax:

Abotel-Tradotel, tel: 47 27 15 15, fax: 47 27 05 87.
Ely 12 12, tel: 43 59 12 12, fax: 42 56 24 31.
Neotel Transeurope Hôtels, tel: 40 44 81 81, fax: 40 44 47 57.
Paris Séjour Réservation, tel: 42 56 30 00, fax: 42 89 42 97.
Prestotel, tel: 45 23 04 61, fax: 45 23 33 94.

Other accommodation
Self-catering is ideal for those who wish to have complete freedom to sample French cuisine in one of the gastronomic restaurants or buy cheese and other specialities from market stalls and tempting *charcuteries.*

Self-catering apartments on short-term lets, called *meublés de tourisme,* are available for a minimum of one week and for a maximum of three months.

The fully furnished one-to-four-room apartments are equipped with telephone, colour television and, in some cases, washing-machine and dishwasher. Sheets are usually provided. Prices are lower for longer lets.

Below is a selection of agencies and organisations approved by the Office du Tourisme et des Congrès de Paris. They are usually open during normal office hours.
ABM Rent a Flat, 115 rue du Bac, 75007. Tel: 45 44 78 79, fax: 45 44 71 22. Métro rue du Bac.
Bed & Breakfast 1, 73 rue Notre-Dame-des-Champs, 75006. Tel: 43 25 43 97, fax: 43 54 47 56, Métro Notre-Dame-des-Champs.
France-Ermitage, 5 rue Berryer, 75008. Tel: 42 56 23 42, fax: 42 56 08

99. Métro Charles-de-Gaulle-Etoile or
George V.
Immovac, 56 rue des Acacias, 75017.
Tel: 47 66 71 65, fax: 47 66 18 96.
Métro Charles-de-Gaulle-Etoile.
Paris Bienvenue, 10 avenue de Villars,
75007. Tel: 47 53 80 81, fax: 47 53 72
99. Métro St-François-Xavier.
Paris Sejour Reservation, 90 avenue
des Champs-Elysées, 75008. Tel: 42 56
30 00, fax: 42 89 47 97. Métro George V.

Bed and breakfast is ideal for those
who wish to get to know French people
and the French way of life. There is a
small membership or registration fee and
the minimum stay is two nights. Prices
are quoted per person and last-minute
bookings are accepted, but not advisable
as the choice becomes limited. The
following three agencies are
recommended by the Office du
Tourisme et des Congrès de Paris, the

first and last being more up-market.
Bed & Breakfast 1 (see address
under self-catering opposite) has its own
grading system and offers reduced prices
for two people sharing a room.
France Lodge strongly advises
against last minute reservations. 5 rue du
Faubourg-Montmartre, 75009. Tel: 42
46 68 19. Métro Rue-Montmartre.
International Café-Couette also
have their own grading system (two,
three and four coffee-pots). Their
membership card entitles you to
insurance against cancellation as well as
assistance towards your return home in
case of emergency. 8 rue d'Isly, 75008.
Tel: 42 94 92 00, fax: 42 94 93 12.
Métro St-Lazare.
For student accommodation and
camping, see the Practical guide (pages
179 and 189).

Sign of welcome at a Marais hotel

Practical Guide

ARRIVING

EEC residents visiting France need only
show a valid passport to enter the
country. This applies to US citizens,
Canadians and New Zealand nationals,
providing the length of their stay does
not exceed three months; a visa is
required for a longer stay. Visitors from
Australia need a visa whatever the length
of their stay. Visas are obtainable from
French embassies and consulates in your
own country; apply two months in
advance in case of delays.

By air:

Paris has two main airports: **Charles de
Gaulle**, 23km northeast of the city and
Orly, 16km south.

Charles de Gaulle airport: tel: 48 62

22 80 (24 hours a day). Roissyrail, the
free airport shuttle service, takes
passengers to Roissy station where they
can board the RER (train every 15
minutes) for Châtelet-les-Halles. Air
France buses leave every 15 minutes to
Porte Maillot, Place Charles-de-Gaulle
and Gare Montparnasse (from Terminal
2). Regular RATP buses run from
Roissy station to gare du Nord/gare de
l'Est (no 350) and Place de la Nation
(no 351).

Orly airport: tel: 48 62 12 12 (6am-
midnight). The new Orlyval is a fully
automatic métro which operates a
shuttle service (every 10 minutes from
6am-midnight) between the airport and
the RER B at Antony station, then on to
Châtelet-les-Halles. It is more expensive
than Orlyrail, which combines the
airport bus shuttle service with the RER
C to St-Michel-Notre-Dame (every 15
minutes from 6am-11pm). Air France
buses leave every 12 minutes for Les
Invalides and gare Montparnasse.
Orlybus run every 12 minutes between
6am and 11pm from the airport to the
place Denfert-Rochereau for connection
with the RER B or the métro.

By train:

The six main line stations are within easy
reach of the city centre by RER or métro.
Gare d'Austerlitz, 7 boulevard de
l'Hôpital, 75013; RER C and métro line
10. Gare de l'Est, place du 11 novembre
1918, 75010; métro lines 4 and 7.
Gare de Lyon, place Louis Armand,
75012; RER A and métro line 1.
Gare Montparnasse, 17 boulevard de
Vaugirard, 75015; métro lines 4, 12, 13.

The métro: clearly marked, clean, quick

Française de Camping et de Caravanning, 78 rue de Rivoli, 75004, tel: 42 72 84 08, métro Hôtel-de-Ville.

These are the most convenient camping sites in and around Paris:

Camping du Bois de Boulogne, Allée du Bord de l'Eau, 75016, tel: 45 24 30 00, métro Pont-de-Neuilly then bus no 144.

Camping International, 1 rue Johnson, 78600 Maisons-Lafitte, tel: 39 62 43 27, 15 minutes from Paris By RER A; information and booking from Euro Leisure France, 11 rue du Tir, 78600 Maisons-Lafitte, tel: 39 12 31 19.

Camping du Parc de la Colline, route de Lagny, 77200 Torcy, tel: 60 05 42 32, RER A to Torcy-Marne-la-Vallée, then bus 421.

Gare du Nord, 18 rue de Dunkerque, 75010; RER B and D and métro line 4. Gare St-Lazare, 13 rue d'Amsterdam, 75008. This station is situated in the centre, in the Madeleine/Opéra district. Cross-channel services from Britain arrive at Gare du Nord or Gare St-Lazare.

By car:
Whether you arrive by motorway or *route nationale* (A road), you will eventually come to the *boulevard périphérique,* which you can follow until you reach the *porte* (exit) closest to your destination.

BABYSITTERS
Three reliable agencies are: ABABA, tel: 45 49 46 46; ABC Service, tel: 45 30 03 22 and Allo Maman Poule, tel: 47 48 01 01.

CAMPING
For detailed information about camping in France, contact the Fédération

CHILDREN
Children under 4 travel free on the Paris transport network and under-18s get into National Museums free. Shopping: babyfood and disposable nappies are cheaper in large supermarkets than in pharmacies. For clothes, try Petit Bateau, 13 rue Tronchet, 75008, tel: 42 66 43 89, métro Madeleine; Mini Club, 13 Passage Choiseul, 75002 tel: 42 96 87 32, métro Quatre-Septembre; or Mouton A Cinq Pattes, 10 rue St-Placide, 75006, tel: 45 48 86 26, métro Sèvres-Babylone.

Gloved traffic police keep things moving

Paris Observatory, centre of research

CLIMATE

Paris enjoys a temperate climate, with moderate rainfall and a good deal of sunshine in spring, summer and even winter. The hottest months are July and August, the coldest January and February and the rainiest season is autumn.

CONVERSION TABLE

FROM	TO	MULTIPLY BY
Inches	Centimetres	2.54
Centimetres	Inches	0.3937
Feet	Metres	0.3048
Metres	Feet	3.2810
Yards	Metres	0.9144
Metres	Yards	1.0940

FROM	TO	MULTIPLY BY
Miles	Kilometres	1.6090
Kilometres	Miles	0.6214
Acres	Hectares	0.4047
Hectares	Acres	2.4710
Gallons	Litres	4.5460
Litres	Gallons	0.2200
Ounces	Grams	28.35
Grams	Ounces	0.0353
Pounds	Grams	453.6
Grams	Pounds	0.0022
Pounds	Kilograms	0.4536
Kilograms	Pounds	2.205
Tons	Tonnes	1.0160
Tonnes	Tons	0.9842

Men's Suits

UK	36	38	40	42	44	46	48
Rest of Europe	46	48	50	52	54	56	58
US	36	38	40	42	44	46	48

Dress Sizes

UK	8	10	12	14	16	18
France	36	38	40	42	44	46
Italy	38	40	42	44	46	48
Rest of Europe	34	36	38	40	42	44
US	6	8	10	12	14	16

Men's Shirts

UK	14	14.5	15	15.5	16	16.5	17
Rest of Europe	36	37	38	39/40	41	42	43
US	14	14.5	15	15.5	16	16.5	17

Men's Shoes

UK	7	7.5	8.5	9.5	10.5	11
Rest of Europe	41	42	43	44	45	46
US	8	8.5	9.5	10.5	11.5	12

Women's Shoes

UK	4.5	5	5.5	6	6.5	7
Rest of Europe	38	38	39	39	40	41
US	6	6.5	7	7.5	8	8.5

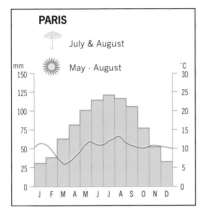

PARIS

July & August

May · August

mm		°C
150		30
125		25
100		20
75		15
50		10
25		5
0	J F M A M J J A S O N D	0

Weather Chart Conversion
25.4mm = 1 inch
°F = 1.8 × °C + 32

CRIME

Do not leave anything of value visible in your car.Watch your bag carefully in crowded places. Some areas are best avoided at night: the Forum des Halles, the gare du Nord and gare de l'Est districts, including the 18th arrondissement, and Strasbourg St-Denis. The métro is safe during the day but it, and the RER, should be avoided after 11pm.

DISABLED TRAVELLERS

Ease of access to sights, museums, theatres and other public places in Paris is improving as the city makes a real effort to welcome disabled visitors. Several brochures on various aspects of daily life are available by mail order directly from local organisations such as **l'Association des Paralysés de France**, Délégation de Paris, 22 rue du Père-Guérin, 75013 , tel: 45 80 82 40, and **le Comité National Français de Liaison pour la Réadaptation des handicapés** (CNFLRH), 38 boulevard Raspail, 75007, tel: 45 48 90 13. However, there is a fully researched guide for wheelchair users and disabled walkers, called *Access in Paris*, available free from Access Projects, 39 Bradley Gardens, London W13 8HE, which deals with all aspects of travelling to Paris and how to make the most of it once you are there: car hire, insurance, information services, train, air and sea travel, accommodation, travelling in Paris, sights and entertainment, emergencies and more are covered in great detail.

Boules in the Bois de Vincennes

DRIVING

Make sure you take your car registration papers and driving licence; an international driving licence is not usually necessary but regulations change, so make sure with your insurance company. Your insurance policy automatically covers you for third-party, but if you want a comprehensive cover you will have to get an International Insurance Certificate (green card). In addition, motoring organisations in your own country propose accident/breakdown schemes to members.

Bane of drivers: vigilant traffic wardens

Road signs are international. There are four grades of fuel: *gasoil* sometimes spelt *gazolle* (diesel), *super* (98 octane), *sans plomb,* (95 octane unleaded) and *super sans plomb* (98 octane unleaded).

A detailed map of Paris which clearly indicates one way streets is essential. Wearing seat belts is compulsory and speed is limited to 50km/h throughout the city, but 80km/h on the *périphérique.*

The *priorité à droite* (giving way to traffic approaching from the right) is strictly observed and bus lanes should be kept clear.

Parking can be a problem and you may decide to leave your car in a long-term car park (ask at your hotel). In the city centre, there are parking spaces along the kerb marked *payant* and ticket distributors near by; the maximum time allowed is two hours (traffic wardens are very efficient). However, parking is free all over town during August. There are also underground car parks at Notre-Dame, Hôtel de Ville, Les Halles, Concorde, etc.

All the major international car hire companies are represented in Paris; they operate from a central booking telephone number, but you can pick up a car from various points in the city.
Autorent, tel: 45 54 22 45.
Avis, tel: 45 50 32 31.
Europcar, tel: 30 43 82 82.
Hertz, tel: 47 88 51 51.

Most of the above also offer chauffeur-driven cars; **London Cab in Paris,** tel: 43 70 18 18 have a fleet of London taxis with bilingual drivers on demand!

ELECTRICITY

220 volts. Two-pin continental plugs can be used everywhere, even in power sockets.

EMBASSIES

Australia: 4 rue Jean Rey, 75015, tel: 40 59 33 00.
Canada: 35 avenue Montaigne, 75008, tel: 47 23 01 01.
Ireland: 4 rue Rude, 75016, tel: 45 00 20 87.
New Zealand: 7 ter rue Léonard de Vinci, 75016, tel: 45 00 24 11.

UK: 35 rue du Faubourg-St-Honoré, 75008, tel: 42 66 91 42.
US: 2 avenue Gabriel, 75008, tel: 42 96 12 02.

Universal sign of frustration: no entry

EMERGENCY TELEPHONE NUMBERS

Police secours (accidents): 17
Pompiers (fire): 18
Emergency treatment:
Samu (ambulance): 45 67 50 50.
SOS Médecins (doctor): 43 77 77 77 and 47 07 77 77.
SOS Dentaire (dentist): 43 37 51 00 from 8pm to midnight.
Burns: 43 46 13 90 (children), 42 34 12 12 (adults).
Poison centre: 40 37 04 04.
SOS Dépannage (car breakdown): 47 07 99 99.
Thomas Cook travellers' cheque loss or theft: 05 90 83 30 (freephone). The Thomas Cook bureaux on page 185 can offer emergency assistance. General travel assistance for Thomas Cook customers is available from Via Voyages, 26 rue de la Pepinière.

HEALTH

EC residents should obtain a form E 111 to enable them to receive the same benefits as French nationals. However, as only 70 to 80 per cent of medical expenses are reimbursed, visitors to France are advised to take out a separate medical insurance.

For residents outside the EEC, cover will vary according to their health insurance policy at home and they should obtain the relevant information from their own company.

HOLIDAYS

On the following days, administrative offices and banks are closed as well as some monuments and museums. Some shops and hypermarkets remain open.

New Year's Day, Easter Monday, May Day (1 May), Victory Day 1945 (8 May), Ascension Day, Whit Monday, National Day (14 July), Assumption (15 August), All Saint's Day (1 November), Armistice Day (11 November), Christmas Day.

Quite a few shops and restaurants are closed during August.

Refuel at un poste à essence

Language

Basic words and phrases:

yes	oui
no	non
please	s'il vous plaît
thank you	merci
excuse me	excusez-moi
I am sorry	pardon
good morning	bonjour
good evening	bonsoir
good night	bonne nuit
goodbye	au revoir
I have...	j'ai...
It is...	c'est...

Do you speak English? Parlez-vous anglais?

I do not understand. Je ne comprends pas.

Numbers and quantity:

one	un
two	deux
three	trois
four	quatre
five	cinq
six	six
seven	sept
eight	huit
nine	neuf
ten	dix
a little	un peu
enough	assez
much/many	beaucoup
too much/many	trop

Days of the week

Monday	lundi
Tuesday	mardi
Wednesday	mercredi
Thursday	jeudi
Friday	vendredi
Saturday	samedi
Sunday	dimanche

Months

January	janvier
February	février
March	mars
April	avril
May	mai
June	juin
July	juillet
August	août
September	septembre
October	octobre
November	novembre
December	décembre

when	quand
yesterday	hier
today	aujourd'hui
tomorrow	demain
at what time...?	à quelle heure...?
where is...?	où est...?
here	ici
there	là
near	près
before	avant
in front of	devant
behind	derrière
opposite	en face de
right	à droite
left	à gauche
straight on	tout droit
car park	un parking
petrol station	un poste à essence
parking prohibited	stationnement interdit
bridge	le pont
street	la rue
bus stop	l'arrêt du bus
underground station	la station de métro
railway station	la gare
platform	le quai

ticket	un billet
ten métro tickets	un carnet
single ticket	un aller simple

LOST PROPERTY

36 rue des Morillons, 75015, tel: 45 31 14 80, métro Convention; open Monday, Wednesday, Friday 8.30am to 5pm, Tuesday, Thursday 8.30am-8pm.

Lost or stolen credit cards:
American Express, tel: 47 77 70 07;
Diners' Club, tel: 47 62 75 00;
Eurocard, tel: 45 67 84 84;
JCB International, tel: 42 86 06 01;
Visa International, tel: 42 77 11 90.

MEDIA

Newspapers:

There are no evening newspapers. *Le Figaro* and *Le Monde* have supplements or magazines on several days of the week, dealing with cultural events, travelling, books, economic and financial

Le Figaro: long-established, conservative

matters etc. In addition there are some excellent weekly topical magazines such as *L'Express* and *Le Nouvel Observateur*.

There is also a profusion of publications containing the weekly radio and television programmes with comments and topical articles on stars and personalities; *Télérama* is one of the best. The whole range of entertainment offered by the capital is reviewed in

detail by two very cheap weekly publications, issued on Wednesday – *Pariscope* and *l'Officiel des Spectacles*. Newspapers and magazines are on sale in kiosks dotted about the city as well as in *Maisons de la Presse* (newsagents), *Journaux-Tabacs* (tobacconists) and some bookshops. Most foreign newspapers are available in the centre, at railway stations and airports.

Radio:

Apart from the national stations like *France Inter* and *France Culture*, there are many local stations which broadcast on FM for the benefit of the Paris region, from *Radio Classique*, the non-stop classical music programme, to *Nostalgie*, a mixture of French songs and light music, and several ethnic stations.

Television:

There are five national channels, three public ones and two private ones: *Paris Première* is a channel entirely devoted to Paris and its region.

MONEY MATTERS

Exchanging currency (notes, travellers' cheques, credit cards) is no problem in Paris; it can be done in banks all over the city or in *bureaux de change*. Thomas Cook travellers' cheques can be cashed free of commission charges in the Thomas Cook *bureaux* listed below, and if denominated in French francs are accepted as cash in hotels, larger restaurants and stores. Thomas Cook *bureaux de change* are located at: Gare de Montparnasse★, Gare St-Lazare, Gare del'Est, Gare du Nord, Porte Maillot, Tour Eiffel, 8 Place de l'Opéra★, and 2 rue Lepic★. Telegraphic transfers of money are available at the locations asterisked.

You can pay by credit card almost everywhere.

OPENING HOURS:

Banks: 9am-4.30pm except Saturday, Sunday and holidays.

Bureaux de change: 6.30am-11pm at airports, 6.30am-10pm at railway stations, 10am-7pm in town. The Thomas Cook *bureau de change* at Place de l'Opera is open in summer until 9pm Monday to Saturday and 10am–7pm on Sundays.

If you find yourself short of cash outside the above opening hours, try a cash distributor. More and more now accept foreign credit cards and have easy-to-follow instructions.

Museums: national museums are closed on Tuesday, except the Musée d'Orsay, the Musée Rodin and Versailles, which are closed on Monday. Opening hours are usually from 9am to 6pm.

Paris museums are generally closed on Monday and free on Sunday (except temporary exhibitions). They are usually open from 10am to 5.40pm.

Shops: most shops open weekdays from 9am to 7pm. Some close between midday and 2pm, some on Monday morning. Department stores are open daily except Sunday from 9.30am to 6.30pm and have a late-closing day mid-week. Food shops open at 7 or 8am and close around 8pm, but they often close for three hours in the middle of the day. Quite a few open on Sunday morning.

Buses use the same tickets as the métro

ORGANISED TOURS
On foot:

The Direction Départementale de la Jeunesse et des Sports de Paris publishes a booklet about various walks around Paris. 6-8 rue Eugène-Oudiné, 75013. Tel: 40 77 55 00.

By bicycle:

Several bicycle hire companies organise trips in and around Paris.
Paris By Cycle, 99 rue de la Jonquière, 75017. Tel: 42 63 36 63. Métro Porte de Clichy; weekend trips. Mountain Bike Trip, 6 place Etienne Pernet, 75015. Tel: 48 42 57 87. Métro Félix Faure.

By bus:

Several companies offer tours of the city and excursions to famous places such as Versailles, Giverny, Vaux-le-Vicomte and many others.
Cityrama, 3 place des Pyramides, 75001. Tel: 42 60 30 14. Métro Palais-Royal.
Excursions Parisiennes, 51 rue de Maubeuge, 75009. Tel: 42 80 42 54. Métro Cadet. You can be picked up at

Train pulling in at Bastille métro station

your hotel; inquire there for details.
Paris Vision, 214 rue de Rivoli, 75001.
Tel: 42 60 31 25. Métro Tuileries.
RATP Excursions (run by the Paris
Transport Authority); departure from
the place de la Madeleine; for free
brochure and information, tel: 40 06 71
45 or 40 46 43 60. Advance booking
from place de la Madeleine, métro
Madeleine or 53 bis quai des Grands-
Augustins, métro St-Michel or Pont-
Neuf.

By Boat:
There are various possibilities for
cruising on the Seine and on the canal
St-Martin, with or without a meal on
board.
Bateaux Mouches, Pont de l'Alma,
75007. Tel: 42 25 96 10. Métro Pont de
l'Alma.
Bateaux Parisiens, Pont d'Iéna. Tel:
47 05 50 00. Métro Trocadéro.
Vedettes Du Pont-Neuf, square du
Vert-Galant, 75001. Tel: 46 33 98 38.
Métro Pont-Neuf.
Canauxrama, 5 bis quai de la Loire,
75019. Tel: 42 39 15 00. Métro Jaurès.
Paris-Canal, 19 quai de la Loire,
75019. Tel: 42 40 96 97. Métro Jaurès.

Outside Paris
Seine Et Yonne Croisieres, quai

Mallarmé, 77870 Vulaines-sur-Seine
(near Fontainebleau). Tel: 60 70 02 43.

Helicopter and hot air balloon trips:
Héli-France, 4 avenue de la Porte de
Sèvres, 75015. Tel: 45 54 95 11. Métro
Balard.

PHARMACIES
The following remain open outside
normal hours:
British And American Pharmacy, 1
rue Auber, 75009. Tel: 47 42 49 40.
Open: daily except Sunday until 8pm.
English spoken. Métro Opéra.
Pharmacie Anglaise, 62 Champs-
Elysées, 75008. Tel: 43 59 22 52. *Open:*
daily except Sunday until 10.30pm.
Métro Franklin-Roosevelt.
Pharmacie Les Champs Elysées, 84
Champs-Elysées, 75008. Tel: 45 62 02
41. Métro George V. *Open:* 24 hours a
day, 7 days a week.

Distinctive green cross of pharmacies

PLACES OF WORSHIP

Information about places of worship and times of services is available from the Centre d'Information et de Documentation Religieuses, 8 rue Massillon (on the north side of Notre-Dame), 75004. Tel: 46 33 01 01.

St Michael's Anglican Church, 5 rue d'Aguesseau, 75008. Tel: 47 42 70 88. Métro Madeleine.

The American Cathedral, 23 avenue George V, 75008. Tel: 47 20 17 92. Métro Alma-Marceau.

St Joseph's English Catholic Church, 50 avenue Hoche, 75008. Tel: 42 27 28 56. Métro Charles-de-Gaulle-Etoile.

Church of Scotland, 17 rue Bayard, 75008. Tel: 47 20 90 49. Métro Franklin-Roosevelt.

Not enough to meet demand: taxis are not easy to hail, so head for a taxi rank

Synagogue La Victoire, 44 rue de la Victoire, 75009. Tel: 45 26 95 36. Métro Notre-Dame-de-Lorette.

Grande Mosquée, 39 rue Geoffroy-Saint-Hilaire, 75005. Tel: 45 35 97 33. Métro Jussieu.

POLICE

The Préfecture de Police, 7 boulevard du Palais, 75004. Tel: 42 60 33 22. On the Ile-de-la-Cité is the police headquarters.

There are *commissariats de police* (police stations) in each *arrondissement*.

In case of emergency, tel: 17.

POST OFFICES

Bureaux de poste (post offices) are open Monday to Friday 8am to 7pm, Saturday 8am to midday.

The main office, 52 rue du Louvre, 75001, tel: 40 28 20 00, métro Louvre-

Rivoli is open 24 hours a day, 7 days a week. The address for *poste restante* mail is:

Poste Restante, 52 rue du Louvre, 75001 Paris RP, France.

Stamps can also be bought in a *tabac* (tobacconist). Post boxes are yellow, free standing or set into a wall.

PUBLIC TRANSPORT

See page 16.

The métro/RER/suburban railway/buses network is run jointly by the Régie Autonome des Transports Parisiens (RATP) and the Société Nationale des Chemins de Fer (SNCF). For general information, tel:

RATP: 43 46 14 14 between 6am and 9pm.

SNCF: 45 82 50 50, between 7am and 10pm.

Passes available in the main tourist office, métro, RER and railway stations entitle visitors to use the whole network for one day *(Formule 1)*, three or five days *(Paris Visite)* .

For information about the Batobus, tel: 44 11 33 44.

Day and night charges are indicated inside taxi cabs; a supplement is due if you board a taxi at a railway station or an airport or if you have more than one suitcase.

Taxis Bleu: 49 36 10 10

G7 taxis: 47 39 47 39; advance booking.

For complaints write to: Service Taxis, Préfecture de Police, 36 rue des Morillons, 75015 Paris.

SENIOR CITIZENS

Whatever their nationality, senior citizens are allowed a discount in some museums and places of entertainment such as cinemas, on presentation of their passport.

SPORT

For details of what is available, see pages 160-3.

Allo-Sports, tel: 42 76 54 54 (from 10.30am to 5pm except weekends), gives information on sports events, clubs and associations.

Waiting at the Gare du Nord

STUDENT ACCOMMODATION

Several youth associations offer cheap accommodation:

Accueil France Famille, 5 rue François-Coppée, 75015. Tel: 45 54 22 39 (apply one month in advance).

AJF, 12 rue des Barres, 75004. Tel: 42 72 72 09.

CROUS, 39 avenue Georges-Bernanos, 75005. Tel: 40 51 37 21.

For information on youth hostels contact:

Federation Unie des Auberges de Jeunesse, 27 rue Pajol, 75018 Paris, France. Tel: 46 07 00 01, fax: 46 07 93 10.

Remember to retrieve your phone card!

TELEPHONES

Calls from hotels are more expensive than from a post office or a telephone booth. Some of these are still coin-operated (1 and 5 francs) but the majority work on a *télécarte* (phone card) of 50 or 120 units, available in post offices, tobacconists and main métro/RER stations.

To make a call from the Paris region to the province, dial 16 (wait for dial tone), then the 8 digit number.

For international directory enquiry, dial 19 (wait for dial tone), then 33 12 and the country code (Australia: 61, Canada: 1, Ireland: 353, New Zealand: 64, UK: 44, US: 1).

To make an international call, dial 19 (wait for dial tone), then the country code and area code (leaving out the initial 0) followed by the number. It is cheaper to call after 9pm during the week, or on Sunday.

To call via the operator, dial 19 (wait for dial tone) then 33.
Reverse charge calls:
Australia: 19 00 61
Canada: 19 00 16
New Zealand: 19 00 64
UK: 19 00 44
US: 19 00 11 and 19 00 19

To send a telegram in any language, dial 05 33 44 11.

TIME

GMT plus 1 hour (winter), plus 2 hours (summer)

When it is midday (winter time) in Paris, it is:
9pm in Canberra;
11 am in Dublin;
11 am in London;
6 am in Ottawa;
6 am in Washington;
11 pm in Wellington;

TIPPING

Service is included in cafés and restaurants. It is customary to tip hotel porters and chamber maids (for a stay of several days), as well as museum guides, usherettes in cinemas and taxi drivers.

TOILETS

There are public toilets in department stores, cafés and restaurants, and coin-operated booths on the pavements.

TOURIST OFFICES

Office du Tourisme et des Congrès de Paris, 127 Champs-Elysées, 75008. Tel: 47 23 61 72. Open: daily 9am-8pm. Métro George V. There are branches at all the railway stations and at the Eiffel Tower.

The Mairie de Paris has a Bureau d'Accueil at 29 rue de Rivoli, 75004. Tel: 42 76 43 43. Open: 9am-6pm Closed: Sunday. Métro Hôtel de Ville.

ACKNOWLEDGEMENTS
The Automobile Association wishes to thank the following photographers, libraries and associations for their
assistance in the preparation of this book.

ALL SPORTS p160 Parade ring (Pascal Rondean), p161 French Open (Chris Cole)
J CRUTTENDEN p4 View from Eiffel Tower
J ALLAN CASH PHOTOLIBRARY p62 St-Germain boulevard, p125 Gardens of Claude Monet
D KEMP p128
MUSEE DE L'HOMME P92
PARC ASTERIX p129
REUNION DES MUSEE NATIONAUX p90
ZEFA PICTURE LIBRARY p75
Anthony Souter and Ken Patterson were specially commissioned to take photographs for this book by the AA
Photo Library, with additional contributions from Philip Enticnap and David Noble.